DAVID CASTRO

THE UNKNOWN GOSPEL

Copyright © 2014 New Covenant Ministries Inc.
All rights reserved

ISBN-13: 978-0692236857
ISBN 10: 0692236856

"Scripture taken from the
NEW AMERICAN STANDARD BIBLE
© 1960, 1962, 1963, 1968, 1971, 1972, 1973, 1975, 1977, by The Lockman
Foundation.
Used by persmission"

*Dedicated to my parents,
Pastor José Gabriel and Elizabeth Castro.*

INDEX
♦♦♦

Acknowledgements... Pg. 7

Introduction.. Pg. 9

Chapter 1
Why I preach the gospel of the kingdom?................Pg. 13

Chapter 2
Religion has deceived the world with another gospel.Pg. 29

Chapter 3
Man cannot solve his problems ....Pg. 85

Chapter 4
What is the "church"?..Pg. 137

Chapter 5
Ekklesía vs. "church" ....Pg. 143

Chapter 6
Kingdom mindset vs. "church" mindset ....Pg. 151

Conclusion..Pg. 169

ACKNOWLEDGEMENTS
♦♦♦

I am grateful to God for creating me to be a vessel in His hands to sow the seed of the Gospel of the Kingdom (government) of Heaven.

Very grateful to the Holy Spirit for given me illumination, understanding and conviction of the everlasting Gospel of the Kingdom (government) of Heaven.

I thank God, for placing men in my life that taught and imparted the principles of the Kingdom, such as: Rick Godwin, Bob Nichols, Kevin Conners, Myles Munroe and Juan Radames Fernández.

For the blessing, guidance and inspiration that my spiritual father Alan Vincent has been in my life, who taught and mentored the Kingdom to me.

Very thankful to thousands of brothers and sisters, that for 39 years have supported me with their love, prayers and financial support.

To Esther García Cano, for the long hours editing, translating and transcribing of this book.

INTRODUCTION
♦♦♦

"But seek first His kingdom and His righteousness, and all these things will be added to you."
Matthew 6:33

For centuries, man has pursued different systems such as dictatorships, monarchies, tyrannies, socialism, democracy, communism, and imperialism, trying to improve the quality of life on this earth. Yet, all these systems have FAILED.

Religion has been the principle basis for more wars, deaths, and division in the history of mankind. Man will fight and die more for religion, than any other cause. Many atrocities and abuses have occurred in the name of RELIGION.

Terrorism, military coups, riots, and activism are simple tools used by religion to further its cause.

It is obvious by today's world condition that man, despite all his wisdom, technological progress, governmental powers, and various religious systems has not been able to bring about world peace, nor a better quality of life.

Religion has hindered man from learning and living The Gospel of The Kingdom (government) of Heaven.

Significance and dominion is about letting you find what religion cannot give you and has never taught.

A fundamental need in every human being is the need to have power (dominion) to be able to control life's many challenges and daily circumstances. Yet, it is impossible to have dominion or power if we first are not under authority.

I have had the joy and blessing to travel to more than 100 countries around the world. I have ministered, and talked to thousands of men and woman from different cultural backgrounds, social-economics, religious beliefs and races. In all of them, I have heard a common cry –people are SEARCHING for answers to life's daily challenges.

To find the answer, we must go back to where it all began and for what purpose. This book is the first of a series of books on the Kingdom (government) of Heaven.

I want to submit to you the source for dominion, power, and authority (government), so you may submit to it, and fulfill the PURPOSE for which God created you.

The purpose of this book, *The Unknown Gospel*, is to bring clarity, revelation, and understanding to the meaning and purpose of the Gospel of the Kingdom (government) of Heaven.

I want to pull back the curtain of religion and expose the misconceptions of this vital topic and attempt to answer questions, such as:

- What is the Kingdom (government) of God?
- Why did God create you?
- Why preach the Gospel of the Kingdom (government) of Heaven?
- What is God's purpose for His Kingdom (government) in today's world?
- Why man cannot solve his problems?
- What is the "church"?
- What is the Ekklesía that Christ is building?
- What is a Kingdom mindset?
- How can God's Kingdom (government) be an active authority in your daily life?

It is my prayer, that as you read the pages of this book, you will grow, mature and embrace The Eternal Gospel of The Kingdom (government) of Heaven and it's Righteousness. Then your citizenship in the nation of God will have purpose and fulfillment.

FIND YOUR PURPOSE... FIND YOUR CAUSE.

In the King's service,
David Castro

CHAPTER 1
♦♦♦

WHY I PREACH THE GOSPEL OF THE KINGDOM

> "This gospel of the kingdom shall be preached in the whole world as a testimony to all the nations, and then the end will come."
> Matthew 24:14

By "KINGDOM" I mean the rule of God with His eternal government over all creation.

This includes understanding that the "church" is not the entire kingdom, but is only in the Kingdom as its primary agent of proclamation and application.

1. The Kingdom (government) message connects the whole Bible and all its covenants to the original Cultural Mandate found in Genesis 1:28:

> "God blessed them; and God said to them, "Be fruitful and multiply, and fill the earth, and subdue it; and rule over the fish of the sea and over the birds of the sky and over every living thing that moves on the earth."

This passage is our starting point; we cannot properly interpret all other subsequent biblical covenants, including the New Covenant, since the Cultural Mandate is the original covenant of creation, which shows all of humanity its purpose.

2. The Kingdom (government) message connects Jesus in His dual role as both Creator and Redeemer:

> "All things came into being through Him, and apart from Him nothing came into being that has come into being." John 1:3

> "He was in the world, and the world was made through Him, and the world did not know Him." John 1:10

> "And the Word became flesh, and dwelt among us, and we saw His glory, glory as of the only begotten from the Father, full of grace and truth." John 1:14

> "For God so loved the world, that He gave His only begotten Son, that whoever believes in Him shall not perish, but have eternal life." John 3:16

Those who preach that the cross is only for individual redemption miss the truth that Jesus died on the cross of Calvary for the purpose of reconciling all things in the created order back to God (*"and through Him to reconcile all things to Himself, having made peace through the blood of His cross; through Him, I say, whether things on earth or things in heaven"*, Colossians 1:20).

3. The Kingdom (government) message brings the "church" back to the overarching narrative (instead of only focusing on various subplots of scripture) which reveals the ultimate purpose of God for the cross and the "church" (ekklesía): the gathering together in one all things under the Lordship of Christ:

> "⁹ He made known to us the mystery of His will, according to His kind intention which He purposed in Him ¹⁰ with a view to an administration suitable to the fullness of the times, that is, the summing up of all things in Christ, things in the heavens and things on the earth. In Him ¹¹ also we have obtained an inheritance, having been predestined according to His purpose who works all things after the counsel of His will." Ephesians 1:9-11

4. The Kingdom (government) message is a generational message connecting the dots between the seed of the woman (*"And I will put enmity Between you and the woman, And between your seed and her seed; He shall bruise you on the head, And you shall bruise him on the heel"*, Genesis 3:15) and the seed of Abraham who would become the "church"

(ekklesía) (*"And if you belong to Christ, then you are Abraham's descendants, heirs according to promise"*, Galatians 3:29) who, as children of God, are called to bless all the families of the earth:

> "¹ Now the Lord said to Abram: "Go forth from your country, And from your relatives And from your father's house, To the land which I will show you; ² And I will make you a great nation, And I will bless you, And make your name great; And so you shall be a blessing; ³ And I will bless those who bless you, And the one who curses you I will curse. And in you all the families of the earth will be blessed." Genesis 12:1-3

Rule as kings in the earth:

> "⁵ No longer shall your name be called Abram, But your name shall be Abraham; For I have made you the father of a multitude of nations. ⁶ I will make you exceedingly fruitful, and I will make nations of you, and kings will come forth from you. ⁷ I will establish My covenant between Me and you and your descendants after you throughout their generations for an everlasting covenant, to be God to you and to your descendants after you." Genesis 17:5-7

"⁹ And they sang a new song, saying: "Worthy are You to take the book and to break its seals; for You were slain, and purchased for God with Your blood men from every tribe and tongue and people and nation. ¹⁰ "You have made them to be a kingdom and priests to our God; and they will reign upon the earth." Revelation 5:9-10

And possess the gates of our enemies:

> "Indeed I will greatly bless you, and I will greatly multiply your seed as the stars of the heavens and as the sand which is on the seashore; and your seed shall possess the gate of their enemies." Genesis 22:17

By implication, this means the gospel message is holistic and applicable for our descendants to engage in politics, public policy, economics, and all the practical affairs of this life that are under Kingdom (government) influence and blessing.

5. The Kingdom (government) message alone gives Christ His proper place as King of Kings and Lord of Lords because every king must have a kingdom to qualify as a king.

To separate the gospel from the Kingdom (government) of God is an attempt to give good news that only applies to the next life.
Hence, it does away with the power of the messianic prophecies that spoke of Jesus Christ's call as Ruler over the nations (read Genesis 49:10; Psalm 2:9-11; Psalm 110:1-3; Isaiah 9:6.7; Daniel chapters 2, 4, 7; Luke 1:31-33).

6. Preaching the Kingdom (government) motivates and releases all the saints in the "church" (ekklesía) to serve as ministers of the Lord in His Kingdom (only 2-3% of all Christians are called to serve in full time "church" ministry). Every kingdom has need for architects, lawyers, judges, educators, sociologists, politicians, economists, social

workers, writers, etc. Understanding this is exciting for every person in the "church" (ekklesía) because of his or her various callings to serve God in the marketplace.

7. Preaching the Kingdom (government) releases Holy Spirit inspired creativity.

The first move of the Holy Spirit was not on the Day of Pentecost but when the Spirit hovered over the formless, empty and dark earth and was an integral part in bringing God's creative order to planet earth:

> "¹In the beginning God created the heavens and the earth. ²The earth was formless and void, and darkness was over the surface of the deep, and the Spirit of God was moving over the surface of the waters. ³Then God said, "Let there be light"; and there was light."
> Genesis 1:1-3

Hence, the Holy Spirit is still hovering over the creativity found in God's image-bearers as we walk out our vocations in the marketplace.

The greatest composers, musicians, athletes, writers, poets, playwrights, and filmmakers should come out of our "churches" (ekklesías).

Universities and education institutions should be founded by Christians.

Harvard, Yale and Princeton were established when the "church" (ekklesía) preached the Kingdom in the 17th and 18th centuries.

Hospitals and the greatest charities should be founded by Christians.

Future mayors, governors and presidents should come out of the Body of Christ because we are called to possess the gates of our enemies and we possess kingship and rulership in our spiritual DNA.

> "⁵No longer shall your name be called Abram, But your name shall be Abraham; For I have made you the father of a multitude of nations. ⁶I will make you exceedingly fruitful, and I will make nations of you, and kings will come forth from you. ⁷I will establish My covenant between Me and you and your descendants after you throughout their generations for an everlasting covenant, to be God to you and to your descendants after you." Genesis 17:5-7

8. The Kingdom (government) is what Jesus, John the Baptist, the apostles and Paul preached and it is the primary theme of the New Testament (read Matthew 3:2, 4:17,23; Mark 1:15; Acts 28:31).

9. The Kingdom (government) message causes the "church" (ekklesía) to be holistic in its approach to ministry because, even by its very name, it challenges us to think of

how we as believers-citizens can collectively steward the created order and manage the earth.

10. The Kingdom (government) message, if received and preached again by the majority of true believers-citizens, would most definitely result in us redeeming cultures, transforming cities, and bringing biblical reformation to whole nations.

Then nations would be spared from either judgment or extinction for not following the pattern laid out in the law of the Kingdom (government) the eternal unchanging WORD of God for structuring nations.

Hence, the only hope for the world is the preaching and application of the Kingdom (government) message. In other words, Haiti, India, Africa and many countries don't need another healing crusade. What these nations need is an apostle of government to become president who will bring Kingdom (government) order and root out corruption.

11. The Kingdom (government) message announces Jesus inheritance as found in Psalm 2:9-11:

> "⁹ 'You shall break them with a rod of iron, You shall shatter them like earthenware.' ¹⁰ Now therefore, O kings, show discernment; Take warning, O judges of the earth. ¹¹ Worship the Lord with reverence And rejoice with trembling."

Where does it say in the Bible that Jesus would have died on the cross if there were only one person on the earth and/or one sinner to redeem? I hear preachers say this all the time.

Jesus died to redeem whole nations and people groups. This goes along with our inheritance as saints:

> "[10] **with a view to an administration suitable to the fullness of the times, that is, the summing up of all things in Christ, things in the heavens and things on the earth. In Him** [11] **also we have obtained an inheritance, having been predestined according to His purpose who works all things after the counsel of His will."**
> Ephesians 1:10-11

It is part of the Great Commission found in Matthew 28:19 (*"Go therefore and make disciples of all the nations, baptizing them in the name of the Father and the Son and the Holy Spirit"*), when Jesus commanded believers to disciple all of the nations, not just individual people but whole people groups.
The discipling of nations was very common in early "church" (ekklesía) history.

For example, when the heads of Gothic Germanic tribes would convert then all of their people converted as well. Whole nations would be baptized.

12. The Kingdom (government) message challenges leadership to become students of God's WORD so they may

have a biblical worldview instead of only preaching the same feel-good, therapeutic messages from week to week in their various meetings and services.

13. The Kingdom (government) message brings back to the fore true discipleship and it challenges every believer-citizen to study the scriptures pertaining to their particular marketplace calling.

14. The Kingdom (government) message makes sense to everyone, especially world changers who come into our "churches" (ekklesías) and feel bored when they are told that the highest calling they can have in life is to serve as an usher or minister inside four walls for the limited ministries of the local "church" from week to week.

Because we have preached a truncated and limited gospel we have lost the greatest world changers–politicians and statesmen with callings like Winston Churchill and entrepreneurs like Bill Gates, Steve Jobs and many others–because they come into our "churches" and only hear messages dealing with life after death.
Thus, they leave and go into the world where their gifts are truly appreciated.

The current religious "church" mindset only appreciates and ordains denominational preachers instead of nurturing and commissioning people called into secular culture as ministers and prophets.

It is a sad thing but, given the kind of preaching we hear in our weekly meetings, many "churches" currently have no place for believers called like Joseph (the prophet economist who saved Egypt and Israel in Genesis 37-50), Daniel (who, as a prime minister prophet brought transformation to Babylon and Persia), or Nehemiah (a politician who rebuilt the walls of Jerusalem).

15. The Kingdom (government) message allows parents to recognize the marketplace callings upon their children and to disciple them in the scriptures accordingly.
Not all of our children are called to be full time "church" ministers but all of our children are called to serve as ministers in the KINGDOM.

16. Those who preach the Kingdom (government) message view the entire Old Testament as relevant today to apply both the moral law (Ten Commandments) as the foundation of judicial law, and its extrapolated 613 civic laws that apply the moral law to specific judicial situations for the purpose of structuring society.

Thus, the Kingdom (government) message causes believers to take seriously the Old Covenant and study it as much as the New Covenant.

17. The Kingdom (government) message causes us to reinterpret many salvation passages from an individualistic application to a systemic and corporate application.

For example, Luke 4:18 connects Jesus as King and announces that in His new Kingdom (government), He will release the oppressed, empower the poor, and release the captive.

In Conclusion, ten Implications of the Kingdom Message:

1. We understand that being born again is not about going to heaven but having our eyes opened so that we finally see the Lordship of Christ over all the earth as King of Kings:

> "³ Jesus answered and said to him, "Truly, truly, I say to you, unless one is born again he cannot see the kingdom of God". ⁴Nicodemus said to Him, "How can a man be born when he is old? He cannot enter a second time into his mother's womb and be born, can he?" ⁵ Jesus answered, "Truly, truly, I say to you, unless one is born of water and the Spirit he cannot enter into the kingdom of God. ⁶ That which is born of the flesh is flesh, and that which is born of the Spirit is spirit." John 3:3-6

2. We understand John 3:16 as not just God loving individual sinners but sending His Son to redeem the created order (the word *world* in the Greek is 'cosmos' which is the systems of the created order).
Thus, God wants us as His Kingdom (government) people to apply the Bible to economics and public policy, not just to prayer and the fruit of the Spirit.

3. The ministry gifts found in Ephesians 4:11(*"And He gave some as apostles, and some as prophets, and some as evangelists, and some as pastors and teachers"*) are seen as equipping the saints for the work of the ministry in the marketplace to fill up all things, and to raise up a mighty unified

army for God. Not just to train leaders for ecclesiastical "church" ministry:

> "¹²for the equipping of the saints for the work of service, to the building up of the body of Christ; ¹³until we all attain to the unity of the faith, and of the knowledge of the Son of God, to a mature man, to the measure of the stature which belongs to the fullness of Christ. ¹⁴As a result, we are no longer to be children, tossed here and there by waves and carried about by every wind of doctrine, by the trickery of men, by craftiness in deceitful scheming; ¹⁵but speaking the truth in love, we are to grow up in all aspects into Him who is the head, even Christ, ¹⁶from whom the whole body, being fitted and held together by what every joint supplies, according to the proper working of each individual part, causes the growth of the body for the building up of itself in love." Ephesians 4:12-16

4. We shift from a platonic/dualistic approach to life, in which we erroneously believe that God only values spiritual things, to a holistic approach in which we value the material world as well (*"And the Word became flesh, and [dwelt among us, and we saw His glory, glory as of the only begotten from the Father, full of grace and truth"*, John 1:14).

5. There is a movement toward incarnation in which we not only "march for Jesus" but we "move in" for Jesus and immerse ourselves in our communities, not just our "churches".

We should serve our cities with our marketplace callings as ministers of the Kingdom, not just serve God in weekly services and events in "church" buildings.

6. The "church" (ekklesía) is to nurture apostles of government, law, economics, and education, not just ecclesial elders involved in "church" government, "church" by-laws, tithes and offerings, and nurturing "church" ministry workers.

7. We understand and view Christ as the King of the earth, not just as the Head of the Body of Christ.

8. We understand that the "church" (ekklesía) is not the totality of the kingdom but is the primary agent of the kingdom as salt and light.

> "[13] You are the salt of the earth; but if the salt has become tasteless, how can it be made salty again? It is no longer good for anything, except to be thrown out and trampled under foot by men. [14] You are the light of the world. A city set on a hill cannot be hidden; [15] nor does anyone light a lamp and put it under a basket, but on the lampstand, and it gives light to all who are in the house. [16] Let your light shine before men in such a way that they may see your good works, and glorify your Father who is in heaven." Matthew 5:13

9. We are to labor not only for revival but societal reformation because revival brings people into the "church" and reformation places believers-citizens in societal leadership.

10. We now understand that the Bible is not really a book about heaven (it says very little about heaven.) but a book about God's KINGDOM (government) and His people stewarding the earth.

Both the Old and New Covenants serve as blueprints for local faith communities to branch out and structure societies with a biblical worldview as salt and light.

Although we believe in the separation of "church" and state because they are two separate spheres of authority in the created order, we do not believe in the separation of God and state because all of life is about religious and moral choices.

There is no such thing as moral neutrality. Either society will be under the rule of an atheistic, humanistic religious order or under a biblical govermental order.

CHAPTER 2
♦♦♦

RELIGION HAS DECEIVED THE WORLD WITH ANOTHER GOSPEL

> "In whose case the god of this world has blinded the minds of the unbelieving so that they might not see the light of the gospel of the glory of Christ, who is the image of God."
> 2 Corinthians 4:4

The truth of the gospel —God's astonishing purpose for man— has been withheld from the world.

Billions are now deceived. Even you have been lied to.

A complete seduction has taken place, and all the world's religions have played a part in it.

Knowledge of your incredible future —your awesome potential— has been kept from you.

Many wonder and worry about the unknown —and what their future holds. Others fear they do not even have a future. Still others fear that civilization has no future.

You need never be in doubt about your future again —or of mankind's.

If only humanity knew, what God has in store for it...

Yet a deliberate suppression of the truth has withheld this knowledge from all but a few. You can be an exception — one of the few who is not deceived.

The world has believed a false gospel for 2,000 years.

It has generally supposed that Jesus Christ is the gospel rather than the Messenger of it. The Message —the centerpiece— of the gospel is not Christ.

By focusing on Him —the Messenger— religious deceivers have been able to successfully suppress and cover up the Message He brought.

The vital knowledge of how man could have solved his problems and understood God's Supreme Purpose has been withheld from the world, keeping it in darkness.

Man does not know what he is or his reason for being. He does not know the way to abundance, peace, and all the good things of life.

The gospel would have shown mankind the solution to its insoluble problems.

And yet, except for the apostle John, all the original apostles were martyred for teaching the truth of God's incredible purpose.

Jesus was crucified because people did not want to hear His Message.

A correct understanding of the true gospel reveals crucial knowledge. It contains a dimension of understanding that cannot be discovered by scientific inquiry.

Every supposed "great religion" of the world has helped suppress it. Their theologians neither comprehend nor are willing to teach it.

We will see that they have held back the great key that unlocks your purpose for being —your awesome potential.

How did this happen? Moreover, who is behind this suppression of knowledge?

To the unlearned, the Bible is a book of shocking statements. It reveals startling truths, completely unknown even to those who profess to understand it.

However, there are few statements more astonishing than that found in Revelation 12:9. This verse directly states that Satan the devil —who does exist— "deceives the whole world".

As *"prince of the power of the air"* (**Ephesians 2:2**), Satan has influenced, guided, controlled, and completely deceived the unsuspecting masses.

This is a staggering revelation —so much so that most simply ignore or reject it, believing that it cannot possibly be true. However, it is in your Bible. And the entire world remains deceived about the fact that it is deceived.

The Bible states that, since his rebellion prior to the creation of man, Satan has greatly *"weakened the nations"* (**Isaiah 14:12**) and *"deceived the nations"* (**Revelation 20:3**) in both understanding and critical knowledge explaining God's purpose.
The Bible also calls the devil the "god of this world"— another shocking revelation.

2 Corinthians 4:4 states: *"In whom the god of this world has blinded the minds of them which believe not, lest the light of the glorious gospel ... should shine unto them"*.

Satan blinds the world to the true gospel for a personal reason. It describes the soon coming Kingdom of God, God's world ruling government. Of course, Satan seeks to block people from understanding this marvelous truth, not wanting "light" to shine on God's incredible purpose for mankind. He wants humanity, collectively, and individually, to think it has no future.

Actually, the devil also recognizes that the arrival of God's Kingdom means he will be banished from his current position (Revelation 20:2-3) of global influence as the god humanity unwittingly worships. He will no longer be permitted to deceive or weaken the nations. He also realizes he can never receive what God has offered to men.

In John 12:31, 14:30, and 16:11, Jesus refers to Satan as *"the prince of this world"*. These verses state that the devil will one day be judged. Take a moment to read them. John 12:31 parallels the judgment of this world with Satan's judgment: *"Now judgment is upon this world; now the ruler of this world will be cast out"*. Why? Because this world is his. Paul's inspired statement reveals that he is literally its "god".

Man's civilization, with its cultures, ways, and systems, is under the control of the devil.

If Satan has deceived the entire world, then this cannot be God's world. And since the whole world is deceived, it is cut off from God.

Deceived people do not know their purpose for being, and their daily practices reflect this ignorance (Isaiah 59:1-2). *"Your iniquities have turned these away, And your sins have withheld good from you"* (Jeremiah 5:25).

We could ask: how can a single being deceive over six and a half billion people? There are two primary ways.
First, Revelation 12:9 concludes with, *"he was cast out into the earth, and his angels were cast out with him"*. Notice that it says, "his angels". These beings, which he leads, are referred to as demons (or fallen angels), and they assist Satan in his role of super deceiver.

Therefore, Satan does not work alone —he has millions of deceived spirit beings (fallen angels) that help him.

However, there is much more to understand. There is a second, equally important way through which Satan has so successfully deceived such vast numbers of people —and hidden their enormous potential from them.

Christendom is represented by hundreds of different, competing, arguing and multiplying denominations, and sects. Supposed Christianity appears in every conceivable shape, flavor, color, and texture of belief and custom. Most have assumed that this is the natural state of affairs in the "Christian" world —that this is the way God must want it. How WRONG they are.

Put another way, this means that there are hundreds of thousands, and perhaps millions, of clergy who represent and teach the beliefs of this kaleidoscope of differing and disagreeing brands of Christianity.

Most who attend these various "churches" have also assumed, therefore, that all these must generally be God's ministers —that they represent and teach what God wants taught. There could be no more dangerous —or wrong— assumption.

Now here is yet one statement that is more shocking. As the god of a completely deceived world, which must, therefore, include all the differing forms of Christianity and other religions, Satan has his own agents. He uses these agents to unwittingly spread his false doctrines.

Yes, he has been able to achieve this universal success because the devil HAS HIS OWN MINISTERS.

Of course, his agents —his ministers— are themselves deceived into believing that they are God's ministers. Some teach a few aspects of God's truth, but virtually none of His most important truths. Now notice 2 Corinthians 11:13-15:

> "¹³ For such men are false apostles, deceitful workers, disguising themselves as apostles of Christ. ¹⁴ No wonder, for even Satan disguises himself as an angel of light. ¹⁵ Therefore it is not surprising if his servants also disguise themselves as servants of righteousness, whose end will be according to their deeds".

The apostle Paul warned of the cunning ways with which Satan's ministers successfully deceive.

This is a blunt, stunning scripture. Yet, it is true that Satan's ministers appear to be the ministers of God. Satan does not talk directly to human beings. He works through his servants —his ministers.

And here is the greatest deception of these false ministers: the devil uses them as instruments for spreading a false gospel about the Person of Jesus Christ, instead of His Message of the Kingdom of Heaven (government) the one that Jesus brought.

The greatest truth that the ministers, theologians, and religionists of this world deny is the incredible potential that each human being carries and the reigning purpose for which God has created them.

The following verses continue Paul's description of the work of false ministers. They demonstrate the ongoing danger of Satan's agents seeking to penetrate the true EKKLESÍA to blind God's true servants a second time to the wonderful truth of the gospel and return them to darkness.

> "But I fear, lest by any means, as the serpent beguiled Eve through his subtlety, so you're [the Corinthian brethren's] minds should be corrupted from the simplicity that is in Christ. For if he that comes [speaking of false preachers] preaches another Jesus…or if you receive another spirit…or another gospel, which you have not, accepted …" 2 Corinthians 11:3-4

Paul warned of "another" spirit that was even able to enter the true EKKLESÍA. This very different spirit perverted both the truth about the gospel and the real Christ of the Bible.
Historically, the counterfeit Christianity of today first appeared almost immediately after Jesus's death and resurrection.

Also, ask yourself: if Jesus is the gospel, then why cite "another Jesus" and "another gospel" as two separate doctrinal errors?

The Unknown Gospel

The New Testament contains numerous warnings of seducers, deceivers, charlatans, and imposters who would try to enter the true EKKLESÍA and lead away followers into false doctrines.

Most of the apostles, in one way or another, warned virtually every congregation of this danger. It is this same system of false Christianity into which most people have been born and spent their lives.

The apostle Peter warned of false teachers "among you [the church (ekklesía)]".

> "But there were false prophets also among the people, even as there shall be false teachers among you, who privily shall bring in damnable heresies, even denying the Lord that bought them, and bring upon themselves swift destruction. And many shall follow their pernicious ways; by reason of whom the way of truth shall be evil spoken of. And through covetousness shall they with feigned words make merchandise of you." 2 Peter 2:1-3

These are strong words. Just as false prophets continually plagued ancient Israel, "false teachers" who, through "feigned words", did seduce "many" into following them have assaulted the "church" through the centuries. The goal was to pull people from "the way of truth".

The apostle Jude, Jesus's younger brother, was equally direct in his warning:

> "Beloved, when I gave all diligence to write unto you of the common salvation ... and exhort you that you should earnestly contend for the faith which was once delivered unto the saints. For there are certain men crept in unawares, who were before of old ordained to this condemnation, ungodly men, turning the grace of our God into lasciviousness [license to break God's Law]..." Jude 3-4

This powerful indictment describes those who "crept in" and caused some to no longer fight for "the faith, which was once delivered". Notice it says that some of these imposters had been "before of old ordained". Because they were ungodly, they taught others to break God's Law as well.

We will examine Acts 8 momentarily to better understand where these men came from. Their system and doctrines are far from new.

John recorded nearly an entire chapter of Jesus's own words of warning to all His future sheep. Jesus pulls no punches when describing the true nature of false leaders and teachers. Here are excerpts from that chapter:

> "He that enters not by the door into the sheepfold [the ekklesía]... the same is a thief and a robber...the Shepherd [Jesus and His faithful ministry] of the sheep...the sheep follow Him: for they know His voice. And a stranger will they not follow, but will flee from him: for they

know not the voice of STRANGERS... Then said Jesus...I am the door of the sheep. All that ever came before Me are thieves and robbers: but the sheep did not hear them. I am the door: by Me if any man enters in, he shall be saved, and shall go in and out, and find pasture. The thief comes not, but for to steal, to kill, and to destroy: I am come that they might have life, and that they might have it more abundantly. I am the good Shepherd: the good Shepherd gives His life for the sheep. But he that is an hireling...sees the wolf coming...and flees: and the wolf catches them, and scatters the sheep. The hireling flees, because he is an hireling, and cares not for the sheep." John 10:1-13

Take time to read this entire chapter. Notice the repeated use of the terms "wolf, stranger, thief, robber" and "hireling" —these latter are those who abandon the flock, pursuing self-interest.

Throughout "church" history, when enemies threatened God's people, most ministers did abandon the flock, and many sheep were deceived and swept away from God's ekklesía and truth.

In addition to the Corinthians, Paul warned several other congregations. Here is what he told the Galatians after they had slipped into false doctrines: *"You did run well; who did hinder you that you should not obey the truth? This persuasion comes not of Him that calls you. A little leaven leavens the whole lump"*, **Galatians 5:7-9.**

The Galatians had gotten off track. They did not understand that a little false doctrine ("leaven") eventually spreads (like leaven in dough) through the "whole lump" of God's many truths. The Galatians were losing their understanding of the gospel.

Now turn to a warning Paul gave to the Thessalonians, in which he spoke of a *"mystery of iniquity"* that was already at work in the first century "church" (ekklesía). The context there (2 Thessalonians 2:3) also contains a description of events that would immediately precede Christ's Return. A *"falling away"* and a revealing of the *"man of sin...the son of perdition"* would first have to take place before Christ's Second Coming. He wrote, *"For the mystery of iniquity does already work"* (2 Thessalonians 2:7).
Paul understood that certain events were *"already"* in play in the ekklesía then, just as they would come to be, once again, at the end of the age.

The Book of Acts describes events in Samaria and sets up more facts to consider *"And at that time there was a great persecution against the ekklesía which was at Jerusalem; and they were all scattered abroad throughout the regions of Judea and Samaria, except the apostles... Therefore, they that were scattered abroad went everywhere preaching the word. Then Philip went down to the city of Samaria... And there was great joy in that city"* (Acts 8:1, 4-5, 8).

Later, several verses reference one Simon the Sorcerer (often called Simon Magus by various "church" historians). This man had tremendous influence in the predominantly Gentile area of Samaria. He was a part of the mystery system of which Paul warned the Thessalonians (also see Revelation 17:5, and later in this book). This same powerful system, originally led by Simon, has continually sought to enter the true EKKLESÍA.

> "But there was a certain man, called Simon, which beforetime in the same city used sorcery, and bewitched the people of Samaria, giving out that himself was some great one: to whom they all gave heed, from the least to the greatest, saying, This man is the great power of God. And to him they had regard, because that of long time he had bewitched them with sorceries." Acts 8:9-11

The Bible explains what "word" Philip was preaching: *"But when they believed Philip preaching the good news about the kingdom of God and the name of Jesus Christ, they were being baptized, men and women alike"*, Acts 8:12. Notice that these in Samaria were baptized only after *"they believed"* this message —the Kingdom of God (government)— not some humanly devised counterfeit idea.

Here is what Paul wrote to the Ephesians. This passage describes various offices Jesus Christ established within His New Testament ministry. It explains the purposes of those offices in edifying, unifying, and perfecting the brethren of God's EKKLESÍA.

> "And He gave some, apostles; and some, prophets; and some, evangelists; and some, pastors and teachers; for the perfecting of the saints, for the work of the ministry, for the edi-

> fying of the body of Christ: till we all come in the unity of the faith, and of the knowledge of the Son of God, unto a perfect man, unto the measure of the stature of the fullness of Christ: that we henceforth be no more children, tossed to and fro, and carried about with every wind of doctrine, by the sleight of men, and cunning craftiness, whereby they lie in wait to deceive; but speaking the truth in love, may grow up into him in all things, which is the Head, even Christ." Ephesians 4:11-15

This is another very strong and instructive series of warnings to God's people. Christ intended that His sheep listen to true ministers and recognize false *"winds of doctrine"* that may be packaged in *"cunning"* and *"crafty"* ways.

Near the end of Paul's ministry, just before going on trial for his life, he met with all the assembled elders in Ephesus. This was an emotional meeting, because he knew that he would not see them again. He took time to remind them of their obligation, and of what he had repeatedly instructed them over a period of three years.

The responsibility Paul described remains for God's true ministry today.

Carefully note how Paul stressed the importance of his having preached the Kingdom of God (government):

> "I know that you all, among whom I have gone preaching the kingdom of God, shall see my face no more…Take heed…to all the flock…to feed the "church" of God…For I know this,

that after my departing shall grievous wolves enter in among you, not sparing the flock. Also of your own selves shall men arise, speaking perverse things, to draw away disciples after them. Therefore watch, and remember, that by the space of three years I ceased not to warn every one night and day with tears." Acts 20:25, 28-31

What Paul had warned of did happen. Heretics entered not only the Ephesians congregation but also most of the rest of God's EKKLESÍA and subverted it into false understanding and practices.

"Church" historians commonly refer to the period from the mid-first century AD to the middle of the second century AD as the "lost century".

During this period, the visible "church" (ekklesía) radically changed in appearance, becoming almost unrecognizable. Remaining true believers, who were in the small minority, were forced to flee the visible majority, which had departed into error.

The knowledge of God's awesome purpose for human existence became lost to the overwhelming majority of those who were swept away into a false salvation.

Ever since the first century, when Christ established His Ekklesía, it has had to fight for the truth. God's people have always had to be careful —extremely vigilant— about the dangers of false ministers coming among them and perverting some or all of the doctrines of God. These imposters always teach a false gospel.

Paul warned the Corinthians that they had been *"beguiled"* into accepting "another gospel" (*"For if one comes and preaches another Jesus whom we have not preached, or you receive a different spirit which you have not received, or a different gospel which you have not accepted, you bear this beautifully"*, **2 Corinthians 11:4**).

THE GREATEST SINGLE DOCTRINE IN THE BIBLE IS THE KNOWLEDGE OF THE TRUE GOSPEL

There is only one true gospel. All others are perversions designed by Satan to replace the incredible truth of its Message. It is this enormous understanding that Satan's ministers always seems to pervert first.

At the very beginning of His ministry, Jesus taught, *"Repent, and believe the gospel"* (**Mark 1:15**). But what is the true gospel? Is there more than one that God approves? The answers to these and other questions about the gospel are found in the Bible —and they are vital for you to understand.

Thousands of new books on religion are published each year in America. And there are over two thousand separate denominations and sects in America, as well. Yet, there has never been more confusion and disagreement among professing Christians, or in the world as a whole, about the true answers to life's great problems. Why?

Why is there so much knowledge available, while at the same time so much ignorance of the truth about life's BIG questions?
The answers to these questions have everything to do with the gospel.

The vast majorities have been taught —and believe— that the gospel is merely about the Person of Jesus. Certainly, Jesus's role is an extremely important subject, but He is not the gospel. The Bible shows that the name of Jesus Christ is preached in conjunction with the gospel. Again, His role is vital to Christianity, and must be understood, but He is not the gospel.

Some proclaim a "gospel of salvation", a "gospel of grace", a "gospel of prosperity", a "gospel of miracles", a "social gospel," a "gospel of foods", a "gospel of deliverance", a "gospel of healing", a "gospel of faith", etc. Others merely think of "gospel music" when they hear this word. These are all teachings that ignore the truth of the Bible.

Let us return to Mark 1, and notice verse 14: *"Now after that John was put in prison, Jesus came into Galilee, preaching the gospel of the kingdom of God"*. Jesus preached this gospel. And it was in the same context that He said, "Repent you, and believe the gospel". Again, what gospel? The gospel of the "Kingdom of God".
Verse 1 refers to this message when it states, "The beginning of the gospel of Jesus Christ". Jesus's gospel was about the Kingdom of GOD (government) —not something else.

One must believe that gospel, not a counterfeit or substitute. The world simply does not know of this gospel.

Why do so few today grasp the awesome future of the Christian calling? Paul was inspired to explain:

> "But as it is written, Eye has not seen, nor ear heard, neither have entered into the heart of man, the things which God has prepared for them that love Him. But God has revealed them unto us by His Spirit: for the Spirit searches all things, yes, the deep things of God." 1 Corinthians 2:9-10

Without God opening the mind, it is impossible to understand any of the things of God. It is also impossible to even come to God (John 6:44, 65). Quite literally, this verse states that God's purpose has never entered man's thinking.

God, for His own marvelous purpose at this time, has opened the truth of the gospel to a very few —and has put them into His EKKLESÍA. The rest of the world remains blinded. Understand this. The devil does not want human beings to enjoy what is forever denied to him —citizenship in the Family of God (nation).

Most will not wake up to the deception —the mass delusion— of a seduced "Christianity" that denies the truths of the Bible.

The Unknown Gospel

God's plan for mankind is staggering —incomparable to anything human beings have devised to replace it. The world ignores, clear scriptures found throughout God's Word about the Kingdom of God. His Government.

This subject is so important that God inspired Paul to issue this warning to the Galatians then and to us now:

> "I marvel that you are so soon removed from Him that called you into the grace of Christ unto another gospel: which is not another; but there be some that trouble you, and would pervert the gospel of Christ. But though we, or an angel from heaven, preach any other gospel unto you than that which we have preached unto you, let him be accursed. As we said before, so say I now again, If any man preach any other gospel unto you than that you have received, let him be accursed." Galatians 1:6-9

This is a very strong statement. A little later, Paul stressed his hope that the *"truth of the gospel might continue with you"* (**Galatians 2:5**).

Therefore, there is one true gospel —with all others false. You can now better understand Paul's warning of Galatians 5:7-9, referenced earlier.

Although some assert that Paul taught a different or additional gospel, it is plain that he never did. Ironically, God used Paul to warn against ever allowing such false teaching by pronouncing a curse on any man, angel, or even any apostle: *"But even if we, or an angel from heaven, should preach to you a gospel contrary to what we have preached to you, he is to be accursed!"*, **Galatians 1:8**.

What a powerful scripture and WARNING.

Paul explained that the apostles were entrusted by God to preserve the true gospel. 1 Thessalonians 2:4: *"But as we were allowed of God to be put in trust with the gospel, even so we speak; not as pleasing men, but God, which tries our hearts"*. That is a responsibility not to be taken lightly.

True ministers must always teach what God commands, not what pleases men (including Bible "scholars"). Therefore, any claim that Paul taught a different or second gospel (usually thought to be about Christ or of "peace") is impossible. He would have literally been pronouncing a curse on himself.

Jesus came as a newscaster carrying an announcement. Everywhere He went He made the same announcement concerning, a world-ruling supergovernment to be established.
When speaking to a group of listeners in the desert, Jesus explained His purpose —His responsibility. Notice how He explained His commission: *"And He said unto them, I must preach the kingdom of GOD (government) to other cities also: for therefore am I sent"* (Luke 4:43).

Matthew amplifies this: *"And Jesus went about all Galilee, teaching in their synagogues, and preaching the gospel of the kingdom (government), and healing all manner of sickness, and all manner of disease among the people"* (Matthew 4:23).

Jesus's mission was to take the message of God's Kingdom (government) throughout the cities of Israel. He was "sent" for this purpose.

In the Old Testament, Jesus was prophesied to come as a Messenger.

> "Behold, I am going to send My messenger, and he will clear the way before Me: and the Lord, whom you seek, will suddenly come to His temple, and the MESSENGER of the covenant, in whom you delight in, behold, He is coming, says the Lord of hosts". Malachi 3:1

Christ was the "Messenger", not the message. His message about God's Kingdom (government) is the very core —the centerpiece— of the entire Bible.

Now compare the passage in Malachi with another in the New Testament:

> "The law and the prophets were until John [only the Old Testament scriptures had been preached until John the Baptist]: since that time the kingdom of GOD (government) is preached, and every man presses into it." Luke 16:16

Remember that, in Mark, Jesus preached the "Kingdom of God (government)" and called it the gospel.

Satan, who knew that Jesus was foretold to preach the Message that he hates, sought through King Herod to kill

Him in His infancy. This is also, why sought to tempt Him in the wilderness (Matthew 4:1-11). He knew if he could be successful in either attempt, he could thwart God's Plan and retain power over the nations of the world.

The word "gospel" is an Old English word meaning "god spell" or good news.
The word "kingdom" is also an Old English term, simply meaning government. We may accurately say that Jesus preached "the good news of the government of God".

We will learn the who, what, where, when, why, and how of this good news and how it relates to the Bible's greatest prophecy.

The word gospel is found 101 times in the Bible. Sometimes it is found alone, and sometimes "of the kingdom" follows it. Other times it includes "of the kingdom of God" or the equivalent phrase "of the kingdom of heaven." Note that it says, *"of heaven"*, not *"in heaven"*. It is heaven's kingdom (government).

Just as kingdom of God means God's kingdom, not the kingdom in God, the same is true of the kingdom of heaven or heaven's kingdom. This is critical to understand.

Throughout the New Testament, the word "kingdom" is found 27 times, "kingdom of God" 75 times and "kingdom of heaven" 34 times. All are clearly the same.

Now grasp this point. The subject of the Kingdom of God (government) the dominant theme in the New Testament is also the dominant theme of the entire Bible. Yet, incredibly, most know little or nothing of it.

The ministers of this world's religious "churches" are ignorant of the true gospel and never preach about it.

Therefore, virtually the whole world stands in complete ignorance of the single greatest truth in God's Word.

THE GOSPEL OF THE KINGDOM GOVERNMENT OF HEAVEN

Also, all who once learned it must constantly beware lest it slip away (*"For this reason we must pay much closer attention to what we have heard, so that we do not drift away from it"* **Hebrews 2:1).**

What evidence is there that other New Testament writers preached this same message?
Peter preached the Kingdom: *"For so an entrance shall be ministered unto you abundantly into the everlasting kingdom of our Lord and Savior Jesus Christ"* **(2 Peter 1:11).**
So did the apostle James: *"Hearken, my beloved brethren, has not God chosen the poor of this world rich in faith, and heirs of the KINGDOM (government) which He has promised to them that love Him?"* **(James 2:5).**

Matthew's account mentions the term "gospel of the Kingdom three different times. Here is another example, almost identical to Matthew 4:23 already quoted *"And Jesus went about all the cities and villages, teaching in their synagogues, and preaching the gospel of the kingdom, and healing every sickness and every disease among the people"* (Matthew 9:35).

In most of His parables, Jesus taught the principles of the Kingdom of God (government). Matthew alone, mostly through parables, makes over fifty references to the Kingdom of God.

Luke records that Jesus commissioned His disciples to preach this same message: *"Then He called His twelve disciples together...and He sent them to preach the kingdom of GOD (government)"* (Luke 9:1-2).

Soon after, He sent seventy others to preach, and they carried the message of the *"Kingdom of GOD* (government)" (Luke 10:1, 9).

John records Jesus's words before Pontius Pilate on the night He was betrayed. This is an important clue to comprehend. Jesus said, *"My KINGDOM (government) is not of this world [this present society]"* (John 18:36).

Recall that Philip, preached the Kingdom (government) to the Samaritans (*"But when they believed Philip preaching the good news about the kingdom of God and the name of Jesus Christ, they were being baptized, men and women alike"*, Acts 8:12). He preached separately the Kingdom and Christ: *"But when they believed Philip...concerning the Kingdom of God (government), and the name of Jesus Christ, they were baptized, both men and women"* (Acts 8:12).

Philip not only preached the gospel of the Kingdom (government), but he also differentiated it from the teaching about Jesus. Take time to read this entire account. Remember, the messenger is not the message.
Jesus is not the gospel. However, He does stand directly alongside it and will rule the entire Earth when the Kingdom (government) is established.

So then, the writer of Acts further differentiates between preaching about the Kingdom of God (government) and preaching about Jesus Christ. While both are vitally important, they are clearly two separate subjects.

We have addressed how some claim Paul preached a "different gospel". They are obviously unaware that it was Paul whom God used to pronounce a curse on anyone who did this:

> [8] But even if we, or an angel from heaven, should preach to you a gospel contrary to what we have preached to you, he is to be accursed. [9] As we have said before, so I say again now, if any man is preaching to you a gospel contrary to what you received, he is to be accursed. Galatians 1:8-9

We have seen that Paul preached the Kingdom of God (government). However, you will notice two verses in Acts, which show that he did not neglect the second subject of Christ's role in the process of salvation.

First, let us establish that Paul preached God's Kingdom (government) to the Gentiles. Acts 19:8 states, *"And he went into the synagogue, and spoke boldly for the space of three months, disputing and persuading the things concerning the kingdom of God (government)"*.
There are many places in his epistles where Paul taught the Kingdom to various Gentile "churches". His message was always the same, continually preaching and referring to the Kingdom of God (government). Examine this from Acts 20:25: *"I have gone preaching the kingdom of God… repentance toward God, and faith toward our Lord Jesus Christ"* (vs. 21). This account makes clear that Paul preached the same gospel —also alongside the role of Christ— to both Jew and Gentile.

Acts 28:30-31: *"And Paul dwelt two whole years in his own hired house, and received all that came in unto him, preaching the kingdom of GOD (government), and teaching those things which concern the Lord Jesus Christ"*. Like Philip, Paul understood that the gospel and who Jesus Christ was, were two separate subjects.

Finally, consider one more passage where Paul made a distinction between the gospel and the Person of Jesus, by briefly referencing again 2 Corinthians 11:4: *"For if he that comes preaches another Jesus, whom we have not preached … or another gospel which you have not accepted, you might well bear with him"* (the margin more correctly renders this last phrase "with me"). Paul urged the Corinthians to reject false teachers and to hold to what he had taught them. He plainly distinguished the teaching of a false Jesus and a false gospel as two separate errors.

Again, ask yourself: if Jesus is the gospel, then why did Paul (four times) and Philip speak of them as two separate matters?

Many have supposed that the gospel is exclusively a New Testament message. Nothing could be further from the truth. The Bible is literally filled with places, Old and New Testament, which describe various aspects and prophecies about the Kingdom of God (government).

Let's consider an amazing statement by Peter found in Acts 3:19-21:

> "Repent you therefore, and be converted, that your sins may be blotted out, when the times of refreshing shall come from the presence of the Lord; and He shall send Jesus Christ, which before was preached unto you: Whom the heaven must receive until the times of restitution of all things, which God has spoken by the mouth of all His holy prophets since the world began."

Notice that Peter refers to the Coming of Christ —*"the presence of the Lord"* **(Acts 3:19)**, with verse 20 stating that God *"shall send Jesus Christ"*. Verse 21 describes God's Kingdom (government) as the *"restitution of all things"*. Peter stated that this "restitution" (Christ establishing His Kingdom-government) is something that *"God has spoken by ... ALL His holy prophets since the world began"*.

Could God have actually used every one of His prophets to announce His Kingdom (government)? Why do Bible scholars and religionists ignore this—or even reject it outright?

Jude wrote that *"Enoch [Noah's great grandfather]...prophesied...saying, Behold, the Lord comes...to execute judgment upon all"* **(Jude 14-15)**. This obviously refers to Jesus Christ returning to establish a government, ruling ALL nations.

In 2 Peter 2:5, Noah is referred to as the *"eighth...preacher of righteousness"*. Jude wrote that Enoch was the *"seventh from Adam"*. Hence, Noah, next to follow him, is referred to as "the eighth". Beginning with Abel, and including Enoch, there were seven men who previously held this role before Noah. These eight men's lives spanned the entire period between Adam and the Flood, and they all preached the same message.

Careful review of Jude reveals that Enoch also preached about sin and righteousness. Suffice to say, all of these men spoke the same message.

Peter said, *"...since the world began"*. Who else preached of God's Kingdom (government)?

Is there evidence that the gospel was preached during the period following the Flood? In Genesis 12:3, God said to Abraham, *"In you shall all families of the earth be blessed"*. This is also referenced in Galatians 3:8, but phrased a little differently: *"...in you [Abraham] shall all nations be blessed."* This same verse states that the gospel was *"preached before unto Abraham"*.

The Unknown Gospel

This is fascinating. Not only did Abraham have the gospel preached to him (almost certainly by Melchizedek—Christ), but it was also preached in Genesis, through Moses' writings, about Abraham. Now consider. How could all nations be blessed unless Christ one day establishes His government on Earth?

While Moses was not a "preacher of righteousness" or an apostle, he was a prophet and a judge, and the first man God raised up to lead Israel. Perhaps you have never thought of Moses as one who preached the gospel. Yet, the Bible reveals that he did, to ancient Israel, when they were in the wilderness. We saw that Genesis 12:3 refers to the gospel, as does Numbers 24:17-19, and both were recorded by Moses.

Acts 3:22 plainly state Moses foretold that God would raise up Jesus Christ as a great Prophet (Deuteronomy 18:15) to preach to the whole world (Acts 3:23) at His Return. Most are only familiar with Moses leading Israel out of Egypt, and are completely ignorant of how God used him in this way.

Hebrews 3:9 and 4:2 also demonstrate that Moses preached the gospel to ancient Israel. *"For unto us was the gospel preached, as well as unto them [ancient Israel]"* **(Hebrews 4:2)**. These verses, with Acts 3, show that this included the period all the way up to—and through—Samuel.

Acts 3:24 references Samuel as also having preached the gospel. Notice: *"Yes, and all the prophets from Samuel and those that follow after, as many as have spoken* [meaning everyone], *have likewise foretold of these days* [the Coming of Christ and God's Kingdom]". These are clear and powerful statements.

Finally, while virtually everyone knows David was a king, almost no one understands that he preached the Kingdom of God. In Psalm 67:4, he wrote, *"...for You [the Lord] shall judge the people righteously, and govern the nations upon earth."* This statement is a plain reference to God's coming government.

The prophet Isaiah made even more plain statements about God's Kingdom (government), about how it would appear and bring peace to all nations on Earth. He also made clear that God's kingdom involves government:

> "For unto us a Child is born, unto us a Son is given: and the government shall be upon His shoulder: and His Name shall be called Wonderful, Counselor, The Mighty God, The Everlasting Father, The Prince of Peace. Of the increase of His government and peace there shall be no end, upon the throne of David, and upon His kingdom, to order it, and to establish it with judgment and with justice from henceforth even forever." Isaiah 9:6-7

The prophet Jeremiah foretold:

> "Behold, the days come, says the Lord, that I will raise unto David a Righteous Branch [Christ], and a King shall reign and prosper,

and shall execute judgment and justice in the earth. In His days Judah shall be saved, and Israel shall dwell safely: and this is His Name whereby He shall be called, the Lord our Righteousness" (Jeremiah 23:5-6; also read vs. 7-8).

As with Isaiah, these verses need no further explanation. Jeremiah gives a plain description of events that could only be described as the period after God's Kingdom has come to Earth. Therefore, he preached the gospel to the House of Judah.

Daniel wrote this:

> "And in the days of these kings shall the God of heaven set up a kingdom, which shall never be destroyed and the kingdom shall not be left to other people, but it shall break in pieces and consume all these kingdoms (governments), and it shall stand forever." Daniel 2:44

Did this prophet preach the Kingdom of God? The Bible answers yes —and we will see later that Daniel preached the gospel in many other places as well.

It can be shown that, in one way or another, all those often identified as the "minor prophets" preached the gospel of the Kingdom of God (government). (Jonah is a possible exception.) Remember, the phrase "the gospel of the Kingdom of God" is not the only way of describing the gospel. Genesis 12:3 and Galatians 3:8 have already shown this.

Review the following verses. In each case, you will find that they refer, directly or indirectly, to the Kingdom of God (government): Hosea 2:16, 19; 3:5; Joel 2:21-27; Amos 9:11-15; Obad. 21; Mic. 4:1-3; Hab. 2:14; Zeph. 3:14-20; Zech. 14:1-3, 8-9; Mal. 3:1-3.
After reading these scriptures, it is obvious that Peter was right, and that *"God has spoken by the mouth of all His holy prophets since the world began. The restitution [restoration] of all things"* (Acts 3:21), which can only occur with the coming of God's government to Earth.

It is crucial to make one final point. Acts 3:21 states, "**God has spoken by the mouth of...**" The gospel of the Kingdom is a message from God.

It should be clear that it is GOD who speaks through whatever kind of servant He is using —prophet, patriarch, judge, deacon, preacher of righteousness, king, pastor, evangelist, or apostle. If a man was truly His servant, God always spoke this same message through him— "since the world began".

As mentioned, Mark 1:1 speaks of *"The beginning of the gospel of Jesus Christ"*. Let us ask: Is the "gospel of Jesus Christ" a different —a second— gospel? Did Paul forget that there was another gospel besides the one about the Kingdom? The answer is an emphatic "NO".

However, most preachers teach that the gospel of Jesus Christ is about Christ, also claiming that He is the Kingdom of God and that the gospel of the Kingdom is Christ. We have seen this is false, and completely unbiblical. The gospel of Jesus Christ is His gospel —His message about the Kingdom of God (government).

We have seen that Jesus was a Messenger sent from God with an ANNOUNCEMENT. It was not about Himself —it was about God's Kingdom coming to reign over the entire Earth. In John 12:49-50, Jesus said, *"For I have not spoken of Myself; but the Father which sent Me, He gave Me a commandment, what I should say, and what I should speak. And I know that His commandment is life everlasting: whatsoever I speak therefore, even as the Father said unto Me, so I speak."* It should now be clear that Jesus functioned as a messenger—as a spokesman for the Kingdom of God.

In John 14:24, Jesus said, *"The word which you hear is not Mine, but the Father's which sent Me".* Jesus brought the Father's message—not His own. Remember, He stated in Luke 16:16 that *"The law and the prophets were [preached] until John: since that time the Kingdom of God (government) is preached".*

Make no mistake. With world conditions nearing the final crises, no human could ever bring about a single, world-ruling government that would work.

The disciples did not understand when Jesus Christ would establish God's government on Earth. He had to explain to them through use of a parable. Notice: *"And as they heard these things, He added and spake a parable, because He was nigh to Jerusalem, and because they thought that the kingdom of God should immediately appear"* (Luke 19:11). This long parable explains that much time would pass before it came.

Before His ascension into heaven, in Acts 1, after a series of meetings with His disciples, Christ met one last time with them. Until the very end, He continued to expound the Kingdom (government) of God to them. However, they remained confused about when it would be established: *"Until the day in which He was taken up...[He was] speaking of the things pertaining to the kingdom of God...When they therefore were come together, they asked of Him, saying, Lord, will You at this time restore again the kingdom to Israel?"* (Acts 1:2-3, 6).

Christ explained, *"It is not for you to know the times or the seasons..."* (Acts 1:7).

To explain in a unique way how and when His Kingdom would come to Earth, God, through a series of visions and dreams, used Daniel (*"As for these four youths, God gave them knowledge and intelligence in every branch of literature and wisdom; Daniel even understood all kinds of visions and dreams"*, **Daniel 1:17**). We will see that Daniel also understood and spoke the same gospel that Christ preached.

Daniel recognized that he was a spokesperson through which God revealed His Master Plan.

In Daniel 2, the young prophet interpreted a dream to the Babylonian King Nebuchadnezzar, who ruled a great empire six hundred years before the time of Christ.

The magicians, enchanters, sorcerers and Chaldeans were unable to interpret what God was revealing; it was only through His prophet Daniel.

God revealed that there is an Almighty God who rules the whole universe. All kings, governments and nations of the earth are subject to Him. Daniel 2:28-45:

> "[28] However, there is a God in heaven who reveals mysteries, and He has made known to King Nebuchadnezzar what will take place in the latter days. This was your dream and the visions in your mind while on your bed. [29] As for you, O king, while on your bed your thoughts turned to what would take place in the future; and He who reveals mysteries has made known to you what will take place. [30] But as for me, this mystery has not been revealed to me for any wisdom residing in me more than in any other living man, but for the purpose of making the interpretation known to the king, and that you may understand the thoughts of your mind.
> [31] "You, O king, were looking and behold, there was a single great statue; that statue, which was large and of extraordinary splendor, was standing in front of you, and its appearance was awesome. [32] The head of that statue was made of fine gold, its breast and its arms of silver, its belly and its thighs of bronze, [33] its legs of iron, its feet partly of iron and partly of clay. [34] You continued looking until a stone was cut out without hands, and it struck the statue on its feet of iron and clay and crushed them. [35] Then the iron, the clay, the bronze, the silver and the gold were crushed all at the same time and became like chaff from the summer threshing floors; and the

wind carried them away so that not a trace of them was found. But the stone that struck the statue became a great mountain and filled the whole earth. [36] "This was the dream; now we will tell its interpretation before the king. [37] You, O king, are the king of kings, to whom the God of heaven has given the kingdom, the power, the strength and the glory; [38] and wherever the sons of men dwell, or the beasts of the field, or the birds of the sky, He has given them into your hand and has caused you to rule over them all. You are the head of gold. [39] After you there will arise another kingdom inferior to you, then another third kingdom of bronze, which will rule over all the earth. [40] Then there will be a fourth kingdom as strong as iron; inasmuch as iron crushes and shatters all things, so, like iron that breaks in pieces, it will crush and break all these in pieces. [41] In that you saw the feet and toes, partly of potter's clay and partly of iron, it will be a divided kingdom; but it will have in it the toughness of iron, inasmuch as you saw the iron mixed with common clay. [42] As the toes of the feet were partly of iron and partly of pottery, so some of the kingdom will be strong and part of it will be brittle. [43] And in that you saw the iron mixed with common clay, they will combine with one another in the seed of men; but they will not adhere to one another, even as iron does not combine with pottery. [44] In the days of those kings the God of heaven will set up a kingdom which will never be destroyed, and that kingdom will not be left for another people; it will crush and put an end to all these kingdoms, but it will itself endure forever. ⁴⁵ Inasmuch as you saw that a stone was cut out of the mountain without hands and that it crushed the iron, the bronze, the clay, the silver and the gold, the great God has made known to the king what will take place in the future; so the dream is true and its interpretation is trustworthy."

This detailed prophecy reveals many things about God's intention to restore His Kingdom (government) on Earth. The verses describe the giant statue of a man made up of four parts representing four different empires (governments) to rule over the Earth.

Verses 39 and 40 describe, three successive kingdoms. These kingdoms would follow the kingdom of Nebuchadnezzar.

These verses show a historical succession of the empires of this world, represented by the different metals of the statue, which were natural kingdoms: (1) The Chaldean-Babylonian Empire of gold, (2) the Medo-Persian Empire of silver, (3) the Greco-Macedonian Empire of bronze and (4) the Roman Empire, made of iron mixed with mud in its final appearance.

The message of this revelation is that these four kingdoms (empires) governed and the fourth kingdom would rule and influence the world, until the Kingdom of God is established on earth.

Note that verses 34 and 44-45 show us a stone "*cut out of the mountain without hands*", this is because God, not man, had formed the "*stone*", "*it will crush and put an end to all these kingdoms, but it will itself endure forever*". This can only be a description of the Kingdom (government) of God coming to Earth.

Many ask what exactly is the definition that the Bible gives of a kingdom. Preachers and theologians have tried to spiritualize and alienate the true meaning of what a kingdom is. They have not carefully examined the definition that God gives.

At the end of verse 39 it refers to these kingdoms "*which will rule over all the earth*". This is not a reference to a nebulous idea of a kingdom in the "hearts of men", nor will it fit in any church or churches. It speaks clearly "*will rule*" (govern), by governments with authority over the nations on earth and more specifically over the people.

Note two important aspects of the huge metal statue that is described here: (1) metal decreases in value as it descends from the head to the legs and feet of the statue. This means that the quality of each kingdom (empire) is successively lower in value than the last. (2) The metal increases in strength as we descend into the body of the statue. In other words, the power and scope of each kingdom (empire) is successively higher than the previous.

Finally, we see that the two legs of iron represent a kingdom that is divided. The Roman Empire was divided into two capitals, one in Rome and one in Constantinople.

The last ten toes were partly iron and partly of clay. The iron cannot be mixed with clay, so this is a picture of the end time instability. When the feet are broken, the whole statue of the man collapses.

We cannot today know exactly when it will come, but we can know that it is close. Now notice Daniel 7:18: *"But the saints of the Most High shall take the Kingdom, and possess the Kingdom forever, even forever and ever"*. Then, verse 22 states: *"Until the Ancient of Days [Christ here, and the Father in verse 13] came, and judgment was given to the saints of the Most High; and the time came that the saints possessed the Kingdom."*
Finally, notice verse 27: *"And the Kingdom and dominion, and the greatness of the Kingdom under the whole heaven, shall be given to the people of the saints of the Most High, whose Kingdom is an everlasting Kingdom, and all dominions [rulers] shall serve and obey Him"* (Daniel 7:27).
Daniel knew that the saints would one day reign on Earth with Christ.

Jesus' first recorded sermon, called "The Sermon on the Mount," states *"the meek shall inherit the earth"* (**Matthew 5:5**). Actually, Christ was quoting David, who had recorded this statement in Psalm 37:11 —another place where David proclaimed the gospel. The wording there is precisely the same. Other prophecies also demonstrate that David himself will one day rule over all the tribes of Israel (see Ezekiel 34) within the Kingdom of God.

Notice three separate verses in Revelation. Christ is quoted through John, saying, *"To him that overcomes will I grant to sit with Me in My throne, even as I also overcame, and am set down with My Father in His throne*" (Revelation 3:21). Also chapter 2, verses 26-27: "*And he that overcomes...to him will I give power over the nations: and he shall rule them with a rod of iron.*" Finally, "*and has made us unto our God kings and priests: and we shall reign on the earth*" (Revelation 5:10).

No wonder that when Jesus was on trial for His life, He added more to one of His statements quoted earlier in the book, "*My KINGDOM (government) IS not of this world if my Kingdom were of this world, then would My servants fight, that I should not be delivered to the Jews: but now My KINGDOM (government) is not from here*" (John 18:36). In this exchange, Pilate had asked Him, "*Are you a king then?*" Jesus answered: "*To this end was I born, and for this cause came I into the world...*" (John 18:37).

Jesus fully understood that He was born to be a King. To Govern and Rule. Jesus's First Coming was to be a great event. Isaiah prophesied of His birth to a virgin: "*Therefore the Lord Himself shall give you a sign; Behold, a virgin shall conceive, and bear a Son, and shall call His name Immanuel*" (Isaiah 7:14).

Before Jesus birth, an angel appeared to Mary to explain God's purpose and what was about to happen to her: "*And in the sixth month the angel Gabriel was sent from God unto a city of Galilee, named Nazareth, To a virgin...Mary*" (Luke 1:26-27).

Beginning in verse 30, Gabriel explains more about Jesus and how He would eventually rule from the throne of David:

> "³⁰ The angel said to her, "Do not be afraid, Mary; for you have found favor with God. ³¹ And behold, you will conceive in your womb and bear a son, and you shall name Him Jesus. ³² He will be great and will be called the Son of the Most High; and the Lord God will give Him the throne of His father David; ³³ and He will reign over the house of Jacob forever, and His kingdom will have no end" (Luke 1:30-33).

Jesus was never in doubt about His life's mission and purpose. This is why He continually preached the Kingdom of God everywhere He went.

Isaiah spoke in more detail about how God's Kingdom (government) would spread around the earth, eventually encompassing all nations:

> "And it shall come to pass in the last days, that the mountain of the Lord's house shall be established in the top of the mountains, and shall be exalted above the hills; and all nations shall flow unto it. And many people shall go and say, come you, and let us go up to the mountain of the Lord, to the house of the God of Jacob; and He will teach us of His ways, and we will walk in His paths: for out of Zion shall go forth the law and the word of the Lord from Jerusalem. And He shall judge among the nations, and shall rebuke many people: and they shall beat their swords into plowshares, and their spears into

pruning hooks: nation shall not lift up sword against nation, neither shall they learn war any more." Isaiah 2:2-4

This identical prophecy is repeated for emphasis in Micah 4:1-3. These passages foretell that God's Kingdom (government) will spread around the world. This is why one of Jesus's parables likened the Kingdom to leaven (Luke 13:20-21), which always spreads until it fills its host. The overarching purpose for your life is to participate in the future spreading of God's government.

Jesus Christ came to be a KING who will one day REIGN on the earth. When He returns, suffering, misery, unhappiness, and all the world's troubles and evils will disappear —and world peace will literally "break out," along with supreme happiness, harmony, prosperity, and abundance for all nations.

No human government has ever been able to bring these things to even one country on Earth. This is the core of the very gospel that Jesus brought.

In the Matthew 24 (and 25) Olivet Prophecy, Jesus was asked about those events that would be the signs of His Second Coming and the end of the world (age). He answered that a number of different trends and conditions would occur first.
One event preceding Christ's Return is described in verse 14: *"And this gospel of the Kingdom (government) shall be preached in the entire world for a witness unto all nations; and then shall the end come"*. The true gospel was foretold to

be preached until *"the end comes"*. This plainly means that someone will be preaching it now, in our present age, because the end has not yet come.

Soon, the whole world will see the fulfillment of Revelation 11:15: *"The kingdoms of this world are become the kingdoms of our Lord, and of His Christ; and He shall reign forever and ever"*.

Jesus Christ was born to be a King who will rule all nations of the earth forever with the help of other spirit-composed kings: *"And out of His mouth goes a sharp sword, that with it He should smite the nations: and He shall rule them with a rod of iron...and on His thigh a name written, KING OF KINGS, AND LORD OF LORDS"* (Revelation 19:15-16).

Matthew 6:33 states, *"But seek you first the Kingdom (government) of God, and His righteousness"*. If you seek something first in life, you had better know exactly what you seek.

So let us understand. The word "kingdom" simply means government. Of course, you cannot have a government without a nation to govern. Therefore, a kingdom is at least one nation with a government.

There are four necessary components to any kingdom:

1- Land, property, or territory —however large or small. In other words, one must have a specific and definite set of boundaries that constitutes the size of the kingdom.

2- A ruler, king, monarch, or governor leading the government.
3- People or subjects living within the territory.
4- A system of laws and rules along with a basic structure of government.

No kingdom is complete without all of these fundamental elements. Most do not understand the most basic elements of the Kingdom of God.

- How does this apply to God's Kingdom?
- Is it a literal, physical place on Earth, with people and laws, presided over by a ruler?
- Is it in the hearts of men?
- Is it wherever you find a particular "church"?
- Is it Jesus Christ Himself?
- Is it here on Earth now?
- Is it yet to come?

Paul wrote that Christ is *"the firstborn from the dead"* (**Colossians 1:18**), and *"the firstborn among many brethren"* (**Romans 8:29**). When connected, these verses show that Jesus is merely the firstborn from the dead, with many others to follow. But when, and into what, will these others be born?

In John 3:3, Jesus said to Nicodemus, **"Verily, verily** [this means truly, truly], *I say unto you, except a man be born again, he cannot see the Kingdom of God"*. In verse 6, Jesus continues, *"That which is born of the flesh is flesh; and that which is born of the Spirit is spirit"*. One must become spirit to see the Kingdom (government) of God. *"Flesh and blood cannot inherit the Kingdom of God"* (1 Corinthians 15:50). John 4:24 states, *"God is a Spirit"*.

Under the Father, Christ leads His Kingdom, which is composed of spirit beings. At His Return, Christ, as a member of the God Family, will have many younger *"brothers and sisters"*, who will have qualified to rule with Him.

Genesis 1:26: *"And God said, Let Us make man in Our image, after Our likeness"*. When referring to himself, the One speaking says, "Us and Our". This is proof that there is more than one Being in the Godhead. In this scripture, the Hebrew word for God is Elohim. This is a uniplural term like group, team, committee, or family. All of these represent one entity, comprised of several members or persons.

We read in several places where Christ said only those who overcome will inherit the kingdom and rule with Him. There is more to being in the kingdom of God than just desiring it. There are qualifying conditions that must be met.
Jesus said to a young rich man who inquired about eternal life, *"…if you will enter into life, keep the commandments"* (Matthew 19:17).

Now what is sin? Since committing it results in death (*"For the wages of sin is death, but the free gift of God is eternal life in Christ Jesus our Lord "*, **Romans 6:23**), should you not know what it is? 1 John 3:4 records, *"Sin is the transgression* *of the law"*. This is the same law that the young rich man was told he must obey to inherit eternal life.

Many claim to be a Christian —to be followers of Christ. They claim to "believe on Christ" and claim to be "seekers of truth", when they do not want the truth of the Bible at all. Notice this long exchange that Jesus had with the Pharisees:

> "Then said Jesus to those Jews which believed on Him [these were "believers"], If you continue in My word, then are you My disciples indeed; and you shall know the truth, and the truth shall make you free…. but you seek to kill Me, because My word has no place in you…. But now you seek to kill Me, a man that has told you the truth, which I have heard of God… If God were your Father, you would love Me: for I proceeded forth and came from God… Why do you not understand My speech? Even because you cannot hear My WORD… And because I tell you the truth, you believe Me not [yet it says they believed "on" Him]. And if I say the truth, why do you not believe Me?" John 8:31-32, 37, 40, 42-46

Jesus continues in the account by bluntly indicting those who would claim to be Christians when they are really *"of* (their) *father the devil"*.

Many assert that they "know Jesus" when they know virtually nothing of the true Christ of the Bible. As He said, they literally cannot hear Christ's words —the truth— though they may think that they do: "*He that says, I know Him, and keeps not His commandments, is a liar, and the truth is not in him*" (1 John 2:4).

The world is filled with hundreds of millions of such "Christians", professing a Jesus, but ignorant of the truth.

Many who are not practicing Christianity find their way into the true "church" (ekklesía). However, eventually they all leave. John continued, "*They went out from us, but they were not of us; for if they had been of us, they would no doubt have continued with us: but they went out, that they might be made manifest that they were not all of us*" (1 John 2:19). I have seen this too often. Many seem to only believe "in" Jesus, not really believing Him —that is believing what He said, and said to DO.

Recall that God said that He made human beings in His "image" and "likeness". This verse means what it says. God created you to become "like" Him in every way. Through His Spirit entering the mind of each of His newly converted children, a literal, brand new spirit life is begotten.
Both the Old and New Testaments make this point absolutely plain. While many have some vague understanding that Christians might, in some way, be "sons of God", few consider this: "*Beloved, now are we the sons of God, and it does not yet appear what we shall be: but we know that, when He shall appear, we shall be like Him; for we shall see Him as He is*" (1 John 3:2). Understanding this staggering knowledge, unknown to almost all who consider themselves Christian.

We will one day have the very likeness of Christ. Romans 8:16 states that we are "children" of God and "heirs" with Christ.

King David understood this a thousand years earlier when he wrote, *"As for me, I will behold Your face in righteousness: I shall be satisfied, when I awake, with Your likeness"* (**Psalms 17:15**). David understood that we would see God face to face. So did John. Both knew that at the Resurrection —when we "awake"— we will be exactly like God, in form and character.

So then, God is actually reproducing Himself in human beings who have received His Holy Spirit. He is creating children that will resemble Him in every way. However, Peter wrote that Christians must *"grow in grace, and in the knowledge of our Lord and Savior Jesus Christ"* (**2 Peter 3:18**). Christians must grow in this lifetime. In order to be given divine authority and power, as joint-heirs with Christ, they must qualify, through the building of God's holy, righteous character in their lives.

First, understand that God created angels to be "ministering spirits" to assist the "heirs of salvation" (*"Are they not all ministering spirits, sent out to render service for the sake of those who will inherit salvation?"* **Hebrew 1:14**). This is their role within God's Plan. Angels are not offered citizenship in the Family of God. This is why Satan (as a fallen angel) so hates the idea that puny, little, fleshly men can receive what he has never been offered nor can achieve.

The writer quotes two places in the Psalms:

> "For to which of the angels did have ever say,
> «*You are My Son, today I have begotten you?*»
> And again,
> «*I will be a Father to Him, and He shall be a Son to Me?*»" (Hebrew 1:5).

God has never said this to any angel.

The writer quotes another psalm, explaining what has always been God's purpose: *"Your throne, O God, is forever and ever: a scepter of righteousness is the scepter of Your kingdom"* (Hebrew 1:8). A scepter is a rod or staff used as a symbol of rulership or authority —and in His Kingdom (government); it is God who has all power.

Finally, the writer re-frames the same question about angels: *"But to which of the angels said He at any time, Sit on My right hand, until I make Your enemies Your footstool? Are they not all ministering spirits, sent forth to minister for them who shall be heirs of salvation?"* (Hebrew 1:13-14).

This sets the stage for what we must understand, the incredible future that God has prepared for all those who serve Him.

An amazing series of verses continues in chapter 2. Quoting David (from Psalm 8:4-6) when he asked the all-important question, *"What is man, that You are mindful of him?"* (Hebrew 2:6). Since God is eternal, and sits over the entire universe and has all power under His control, it is no wonder David asked, and it is repeated, this most central question of life.

The astounding answer begins in the next verse: *"You made him [man] a little lower than the angels; You crowned him with glory and honor, and did set him over the works of Your hands"* (Hebrew 2:7).

God will eventually share rulership of His entire creation with His sons. Again, Christ is merely the first of many sons. The birth of a firstborn son does not preclude the birth of additional sons (and daughters) to that same family. I have two sons and am a firstborn son with a younger sister. My father was a second born son, having an elder brother and so on.

Hebrews goes on to explain that God plans to give enormous power and authority to His Sons: *"You have put all things in subjection under his feet. For in that He put all in subjection under him, He left nothing that is not put under him. But now we see not yet all things put under him"* **(Hebrew 2:8).** This has not yet happened—but it will soon.

When God says that "all things" will be put under the feet of man that is what He means. The vast universe, with all of its quadrillions of stars and one trillion galaxies, will be put under the authority of men who have been born into the Family of God. In fact, the Moffatt translation of the Bible renders the Greek word for "all things" as "the universe".

Before continuing, consider a verse about another related aspect of salvation many have not yet understood. However, the entirety of creation is also intensely waiting the appearing of those new sons to be added to God's Family.

Carefully read the following verses:

> "[19] For the anxious longing of the creation waits eagerly for the revealing of the sons of God. [20] For the creation was subjected to futility, not willingly, but because of Him who subjected it, in hope [21] that the creation itself also will be set free from its slavery to corruption into the freedom of the glory of the children of God. [22] For we know that the whole creation groans and suffers the pains of childbirth together until now. [23] And not only this, but also we ourselves, having the first fruits of the Spirit, even we ourselves groan within ourselves, waiting eagerly for our adoption as sons, the redemption of our body." Romans 8:19-23

All future "sons of God" will eventually be liberators of a creation now in bondage, and foretold to grow much worse. A decayed and wounded Earth, sun, moon, and stars —the universe — will soon be renewed and returned to a state of beauty, harmony, and tranquility under the leadership of Christ and the resurrected saints. Now we can continue the all-important account in Hebrews 2:

> "But we see Jesus, who was made a little lower than the angels for the suffering of death,

crowned with glory and honor; that He by the grace of God should taste death for every man. For it became Him, for whom are all things, and by whom are all things, in bringing many sons unto glory, to make the Captain of their salvation perfect through sufferings." Hebrew 2:9-10

This passage reveals the staggering potential planned for all Christians. When Christ returns, Hebrews reveals that it will be "many sons" who are brought "unto glory" through the *"Captain of our salvation"*.

Verse 11 states that Christ *"is not ashamed to call them* [the other many sons—us] *brethren"*. These are all those of whom Christ is called the "firstborn". Truly, the begotten person has been called to "glory" and to be one of "many sons". Christ's suffering and sacrifices allow Him to be the *"Captain of their salvation"* —and potentially yours.

What an awesome potential for those Christ call "brethren". Now notice this final verse: *"For both He that sanctifies and they who are sanctified are all of one: for which cause He is not ashamed to call them brethren"* (Hebrew 2:11). Christ and the saints share the same salvation.

This verse shows that Christians are "sanctified" (set apart). How? John stated, *"Sanctify them* [begotten Christians] *through Your truth: your word is truth"* (John 17:17).

The cherished traditions and fables of men, about life after death or anything else, collapse under scrutiny. Christians, having come out of a deceived, confused world, are set apart from the world by the truth.

If Christ is *"not ashamed to call them* (us) *brethren"*, then we, God's begotten sons, must not be ashamed to defend the very truth that sanctifies us —and the truth of the gospel (*"the former proclaim Christ out of selfish ambition rather than from pure motives, thinking to cause me distress in my imprisonment"*, **Philippians 1:17**). We must *"grow up"* unto Christ (*"until we all attain to the unity of the faith, and of the knowledge of the Son of God, to a mature man, to the measure of the stature which belongs to the fullness of Christ"*, **Ephesians 4:13**) and hold to the true doctrines of God. We must qualify to one-day stand beside Christ over *"all things"*.

Now step back. Do you see what is described here? The incredible goal of a Christian is to be born into the Kingdom of God—to become a new creation by the spirit, RULING under Christ, as a very Son of God. What could be more wonderful —more glorious— for a Christian!

Matthew 24:27 states that when Christ returns, His Coming will be like lightning shining from the east to the west. This will be an Earth-shattering event, impossible to miss.

Daniel spoke of Christ coming in the *"clouds of heaven"* (Daniel 7:13). God officially grants Him authority to rule the world:

> "And there was GIVEN Him [Christ] dominion, and glory, and a kingdom, that all people,

nations, and languages, should serve Him: His dominion is an everlasting dominion, which shall not pass away, and His kingdom that which shall not be destroyed" (Daniel 7:14).

However, the Christian's responsibility in this life is to manifest God's Kingdom (government). No wonder Christ stated, *"And he that overcomes, and keeps My works unto the end, to him will I give power over the nations: and He shall rule them with a rod of iron ... even as I received of My Father"* (Revelation 2:26-27) and a few verses later: *"To him that overcomes will I grant to sit with Me in My throne..."* (Revelation 3:21).

Sadly, today many do not want Christ to rule over their lives and souls. They want salvation in Jesus but not the government of Christ.

Authority will not be given to anyone who first isn't ruled by Christ. No one can be part of the global government of God, unless he is submitted to God's government.

Most people are familiar with what it's called "The Lord's Prayer". Many recite this prayer often, without having understanding of what they are saying.

This prayer begins, "*Our Father who is in heaven, Hallowed be Your name. Your kingdom come. Your will be done, On earth as it is in heaven*" (Matthew 6:9-10). Of the millions who pray this prayer and repeat it many times, how many really know the meaning of "Your kingdom come" (government or master plan) and rule here on Earth?

For over 2000 years, many have followed the instruction of Jesus in reciting the prayer, without reflecting on the true meaning behind this phrase (*"Your kingdom come"*).

God desires that His will be done in us every moment of our lives. For this to be achieved, He must RULE our whole being.

> **THE KINGDOM (GOVERNMENT) OF GOD IS NOT SOMETHING THAT DESCENDS, BUT A DOMINION THAT GOVERNS NOW.**

Where is your trust and faith? In the principles of the Word of God? Or the traditions of men, that have been influenced by religious systems, paganism, deception, wisdom of men and doctrines that have not brought life, but confusion and destruction? These teachings have been called Christianity and today are the popular belief of the religious "church".

These religious traditions have influenced Christians to not be governed by God, and thus not fulfill His eternal purpose.

The Gospel of the Kingdom (government) of God is UNKNOWN.

> **THIS IS THE HOUR FOR THE GOSPEL THAT JESUS AND THE APOSTLES PREACHED, AND THAT THE PROPHETS PROPHESIED, TO BE RESTORED IN THE HEARTS OF THE SONS OF GOD!**

CHAPTER 3
♦♦♦

MAN CANNOT SOLVE HIS PROBLEMS

> "I know, O Lord, that a man's way is not in himself, Nor is it in a man who walks to direct his steps."
> Jeremiah 10:23

The world is filled with problems, disease, pollution, poverty, ignorance, religious confusion, war, terrorism, crime, violence, hunger, immorality, slavery, oppression, political upheaval, and much more. Why? With the passing of time come more problems, not fewer. Why? Also, existing problems grow collectively worse instead of better. Why? At every turn, man has bungled and botched all efforts to solve his truly great problems? Why?

At the same time, individually, people have never seemed more incapable of addressing and overcoming their personal problems.

As with the world in general, the passing of time finds individuals and families drowning under an ever-greater sea of decadence and seemingly insurmountable difficulties.

In the long ribbon of history, life has been one long stained and tangled mess. We must have thought we had it better because man had improved. However, man does not really 'improve', does he? Man is man. Human nature is human nature; the impulse to destroy coexists with the desire to build and create and make better.

Educators have duped generations into believing the evolutionary lie. This has caused countless millions to believe that mankind is continually evolving into a better and higher order of existence.

Look around and you will see the fruits of this great deception. Man is not evolving upward, he is degenerating downward, into ever new lows of indulgence, decadence, and immorality.

How did civilization get into the state of confusion, division, war, competition, and disagreement that exists all over the earth today? God's original command to Adam was, *"but from the tree of the knowledge of good and evil you shall not eat, for in the day that you eat from it you shall surely die"* (Genesis 2:17).

In the next chapter (*"When the woman saw that the tree was good for food, and that it was a delight to the eyes, and that the tree was desirable to make one wise, she took from its fruit and ate; and she gave also to her husband with her, and he ate"*,

Genenesis 3:6), the woman, with Adam following, rebelled and ate of this wrong tree. Notice that this tree represented knowledge that was both "good and evil". In other words, the tree was not entirely evil—it contained a mixture of true and false knowledge.

It is the same with the "churches" of this world. Some do have small amounts of true ("good") doctrinal "knowledge", mixed with much false ("evil") doctrinal "knowledge".

However, God has always told His true servants to avoid mixing truth with error. He warned Adam that eating of the wrong tree would result in death. It did. The warning is the same for us today.

Consider this analogy: Think of a delicious cake laced with arsenic, cyanide, ricin, or strychnine, while otherwise containing nothing but good and healthy ingredients. Eating the cake would always result in death.

The good ingredients would not be sufficient to overcome the poison hidden in the cake. Likewise, God's EKKLESÍA does not and cannot mix truth with error. As with the cake, the result for those who do is deadly.

Everyone understands the law of gravity. All recognize that if they break this law, it could "break" them. If one accidentally drops a brick on his foot, the result could be broken bones. If a skydiver jumps from an airplane, and the parachute fails to open, the result is certain death. This is easy to understand.

Here are some examples that are only a little less obvious, but are just as true:

- If a person is constantly sick, it is obvious that laws of health (proper diet, enough exercise, or sufficient sleep, etc.) are being broken. Bad health has one or more causes.
- If a marriage ends in divorce, it can also be attributed to one or more causes: lack of communication, financial woes, death of a child, sexual problems, unhappiness on the job, infidelity, etc.
- If someone is pulled over for drunk driving, it is easy to see the cause.

While most never identify cause and effect as an immutable law governing almost every action in life, they are at least generally aware that it is a principle at work in certain circumstances.

However, every effect can be traced to one or more causes. Unwanted or illegitimate pregnancies, crime, drug addiction, bankruptcy, and a thousand other effects, can all be linked to specific causes. Create your own list. You may find it to be almost endless.

The Bible teaches, "*Like a sparrow in its flitting, like a swallow in its flying, So a curse without cause does not alight* [COME]" (**Proverbs 26:2**). Two other translations of this verse are "*... the undeserved curse will never hit its mark*" (Jerusalem Bible), and "*...the baseless curse never goes home*" (Moffatt).

This scripture is saying that every difficulty carries a reason, there is a cause for every effect.

- Why can man not see this law at work when he looks at the world as a whole?
- Why it is that no one is looking for the cause of this world's ills and evils?
- Why are educators not teaching this greatest of all principles?
- Why aren't we concerned as we look at the world around us?
- Why is the world filled with misery, unhappiness, and discontent?
- Why has even the Christian religion ignored this important relationship between cause and effect?

The cause of all the world's troubles began in the Garden of Eden.

The world has lost sight of a decision made by Adam and the woman. They chose not to eat of the Tree of Life, choosing instead to eat of the tree of the knowledge of good and evil.

Have you ever wondered what would have happened if those two people had chosen the Tree of Life? Think of how this would have changed the entire world. Everything would be different.

There would be no armies, wars, death, devastation, or displacement of peoples. There would be no famine or hunger because there would be plenty of food for everyone. There would be no doctors, because there would be no illness. None of the hospitals and clinics would ever have existed. Neither would the prisons, jails, judges, courts, and police forces that exist to punish lawbreakers.

Happiness, abundance, prosperity, and peace would have been experienced worldwide. All people would get along—neighbors, families, individuals, and nations. Can you imagine such a world?

When Adam and the woman made the wrong choice, it directly affected you and me. They brought untold effects upon humanity, because of their single wrong cause.

Let us examine a big reason violating the law of cause and effect that has beset the world with insoluble problems: *"7 because the mind set on the flesh is hostile toward God; for it does not subject itself to the law of God, for it is not even able to do so, 8 and those who are in the flesh cannot please God"* (Romans 8:7-8). Other translations use the stronger phrase *"is the enemy of God"* in place of *"is hostile toward God"*. For those who will believe it, this single passage offers startling insight into the working of the physical "carnal" mind of every human being. Cut off from God, the natural mind is God's enemy —it hates Him.

This verse says that the natural mind does not want, and even hates, to yield to God and obey His Law. While most people profess that they "love God", the truth is that their minds despise His Way and refuse to truly submit to Him, to His authority over their lives.

No wonder Jeremiah wrote, *"I know, O Lord, that a man's way is not in himself, nor is it in a man who walks to direct his steps"* (Jeremiah 10:23). When confronted with problems or important decisions, men simply do not know what to do. They are at a loss for how to correctly address and solve the challenges, difficulties, and problems they face in their personal lives.

How then can they solve the far more complex problems engulfing civilization today? They cannot.

SOLUTIONS BORN OF HUMAN REASONING ALWAYS GENERATE MORE PROBLEMS

Nothing can be understood or accomplished without proper knowledge. Even something as simple as changing a tire requires "know how".

Without right knowledge, mankind stands completely powerless —helpless— before his problems. Because man has rejected the source of right knowledge, he is surrounded by terrible troubles.

Consider just one world problem that has defied all humanly devised solutions throughout recorded history: finding PEACE. Man has literally barred himself from the knowledge that would make this possible. Just look at the daily newspaper headlines. War seems to literally grip the planet in every part of the world.

This is because the governments of men simply do not work. They have never succeeded in finding permanent solutions to civilization's problems. They lack the essential knowledge necessary to solve them. They do not have the answers to mankind's greatest questions.

Man does not, of himself, understand the path to peace or, for that matter, the path to abundance, happiness, health, and prosperity. The greatest thinkers, leaders, educators and scientists have failed miserably in their quest for peace on Earth.

Is it any wonder God inspired the prophet Hosea to record, *"My people are destroyed for lack of knowledge. Because you have rejected knowledge, I also will reject you from being My priest. Since you have forgotten the law of your God, I also will forget your children"* (**Hosea 4:6**)?

Mankind could have known, understood, and had access to far more important, vital knowledge about how to live, but chose to reject it. As a result, God rejected —cut off— man from access to Him (*"So He drove the man out; and at the east of the garden of Eden He stationed the cherubim and the flaming sword which turned every direction to guard the way to the tree of life"*, **Genesis 3:24**). And this cuts men off from the very solutions to the terrible, worsening problems that they now have.

Your human existence is literally a matter of life or death. Jesus said, *"...I came that they may have life, and have it abundantly"* (**John 10:10**). Yet, Paul wrote, *"For all have sinned"* (**Romans 3:23**) and *"the wages of sin is death"* (**Romans 6:23**). Remember, human beings do not have souls; they are souls (*"Then the Lord God formed man of dust from *the ground, and breathed into his nostrils the breath of life; and man became a living being* [soul]" Genesis 2:7).

Man is not naturally headed toward eternal life, but rather toward death. Human beings live approximately 70 to 80 years and in some parts of the world much less. A few manage to live longer than this, but eventually all die. Yet, it was never God's original purpose that it be this way. God wants us to experience life for all eternity.

In 1 Corinthians 2 it says, *"But a natural man does not accept the things of the Spirit of God, for they are foolishness to him; and he cannot understand them, because they are spiritually appraised"* (v. 14). It is simply not possible for human beings without God's Spirit to understand spiritual knowledge —spiritual understanding.

Such things can only seem "foolish" to a mind that cannot "spiritually discern." No matter how intelligent or talented a person may be, without the Spirit of God, it can be said that they have a spiritual IQ of ZERO.

None of the problems common to individuals or nations can be properly addressed and resolved without the involvement of the Holy Spirit at work in minds.

Even attempting to tell people that they lack this spiritual component is a useless exercise, if God is not opening their minds *("*[44] *No one can come to Me unless the Father who sent Me draws him; and I will raise him up on the last day [...]* [65] *And He was saying, "For this reason I have said to you, that no one can come to Me unless it has been granted him from the*

Father", **John 6:44, 65**). It will seem foolish to them, because even this information is "spiritually discerned". The more intelligent and self-reliant the person is, the more foolish it will probably seem to him to be told that his mind is incomplete.

If Adam had eaten of the Tree of Life, he would have learned the way of love —the "give" way—instead of the way of "get", practiced by this world.

The Bible teaches, *"love is the fulfillment of the law"* (**Romans 13:10**), and that *"the love of God has been poured out within our hearts through the Holy Spirit who was given to us"* (**Romans 5:5**). Romans 8:6 states, *"For the mind set on the flesh is death, but the mind set on the Spirit is life and peace"*.

Let us return to the garden. Satan was lying in wait there for "baby" Adam and the woman. Adam and the woman just thought they were grown-up enough to make their own choices. Like most children today, this couple chose not to listen to their Parent, God. Instead, they believed Satan's lie that they would not "surely die".

Cut off from God by sin, mankind has believed the lies of the god of this world since Creation.

> "[1] Behold, the Lord's hand is not so short that it cannot save; nor is His ear so dull that it cannot hear. [2] But your iniquities have made a separation between you and your God, and your sins

have hidden *His* face from you so that He does not hear." Isaiah 59:1-2

"Your iniquities have turned these away, and your sins have withheld good from you." Jeremiah 5:25

Under the influence of Satan, man has practiced sin and disobedience to God's commands and government for all this time. He has tried to treat and correct all of the ill effects instead of dealing with the cause —breaking the commandments of God's Government. Thus, God is patiently letting man learn bitter lessons. The vast majority, who have never known the precious truth of God, have to learn that their own ways do not work.

God is reproducing Himself by putting Himself into each person that He begets. Through repentance and baptism, one receives the gift of the Holy Spirit (*"Peter said to them, "Repent, and each of you be baptized in the name of Jesus Christ for the forgiveness of your sins; and you will receive the gift of the Holy Spirit"*, Acts 2:38), after having been called by God to inherit the promise of salvation (*"For the promise is for you and your children and for all who are far off, as many as the Lord our God will call to Himself"*, Acts 2:39).

Peter, the one speaking in Acts 2:16-17(*"¹⁶ but this is what was spoken of through the prophet Joel: ¹⁷ 'And it shall be in the last days,' God says, 'That I will pour forth of My Spirit on all mankind; And your sons and your daughters shall prophesy, And your young men shall see visions, And your old men shall dream dreams"*), referred to the prophet Joel foretelling a time when God would *"pour out* [His] *Spirit on all man-*

kind" (Joel 2:28). That began with the birth of the New Testament EKKLESÍA on Pentecost in AD 31.

The religious "churches" of this world do not understand anything of the true path to salvation (deliverance). They do not even realize what true salvation (deliverance) is. Only the EKKLESÍA that Christ builds and rules understands these points.

Jesus did not come to save the world now. He has never been on the "soul-saving mission" many have assumed.

> "[22] And He put all things in subjection under His feet, and gave Him as head over all things to the ekklesía, [23] which is His body, the fullness of Him who fills all in all." Ephesians 1:22-23
> "He is also head of the body, the ekklesía; and He is the beginning, the firstborn from the dead, so that He Himself will come to have first place in everything." Colossians 1:18

The false Christianity of this world is blinded to God's truth and plan. Instead of obeying God, millions have been deceived into accepting the ideas and traditions of men. Jesus said, "*[7] But in vain do they worship Me, teaching as doctrines the precepts of men. [8] Neglecting the commandment of God, you hold the tradition of men*" (Mark 7:7-8).

We have seen that human nature is hostile to God. It hates the truth, law, government, and way of God. It does not want to be ruled by anyone or anything. It wants the freedom to follow its own way —believe its own ideas, customs, and traditions— without interference from God.

If one is interested in obeying God, it is only because he has been "drawn" (*"No one can come to Me unless the Father who sent Me draws him; and I will raise him up on the last day"*, **John 6:44**) by God's Spirit and called (*"For many are called, but few are chosen"*, **Matthew 22:14**) to understand His marvelous truth. His eyes are opened to his incredible human potential. As a result, he wants to live a completely different way of life.

Judgment is now on the "church", not on the world. Peter wrote to the "church", *"For it is time for judgment to begin with the household of God* [the church]" (**1 Peter 4:17**).

Eventually, the entire world will learn the truth (*"They will not hurt or destroy in all My holy mountain, For the earth will be full of the knowledge of the Lord as the waters cover the sea"*, **Isaiah 11:9**), with all nations having access to the Gospel of the Kingdom (government). However, that time has not yet come for humanity at large.

The focus of God's plan of reconciliation, forgiveness of sins, overcoming, character development, and receiving the gift of eternal life is focused entirely on the EKKLESIA in this age. Those called at this time must overcome the devil, the pull of this world, and their human flesh, just as Christ did, in order to be part of the Kingdom (government) of God—to be able to rule with Christ.

Armed with this overview of knowledge, Christians are not activists —politically, socially, or spiritually— as so many professing Christians are taught, then thinking they can and should "fix the world", They do not try to "bring the Kingdom" through human effort. They know that only God can bring His Kingdom (government) to Earth. If men could accomplish this, it would be the "kingdom of men" not the Kingdom of God.

God's true servants live with the knowledge of how the true gospel of the Kingdom (government) of God spells the way to ultimate world peace, happiness, health, and universal prosperity. They understand the certainty that the Kingdom (government) of God will solve ALL the world's most difficult problems.

True Christians know what lies ahead for civilization—including both the short-term bad news and the long-term good news. They understand prophecy and do not take matters into their own hands, thereby effectively seeking to neutralize God's purpose, which is to show man that he is utterly incapable of governing himself or solving his problems without the Holy Spirit.

Unease and uncertainty are growing around the world. More and more now ask, "What's happening? Where is everything going?"

How badly is man botching his efforts to solve his problems? So badly that, without intervention by Almighty God in the affairs of men, all human life on Earth would soon be erased—wiped out. Pollution, food and water shortages,

The Unknown Gospel

disease, and the use of weapons of mass destruction would bring mankind to extinction. Mercifully, God will not allow events to go that far. His great purpose and plan is working precisely on time toward a happy and peaceful end —a solving of all humanity's troubles.

Recall once again Christ's promise, *"I will build My church* (ekklesía)" (Matthew 16:18). No matter how men interpret it, this verse speaks of an EKKLESÍA. Christ continued, *"And the gates of hell* [authority] *shall not prevail against it"*. He promised that His EKKLESÍA could never be destroyed.

Over 2,000 different professing Christian "churches" organizations have been "built" by men, just in the United States. Another is started every three days. Estimates place the number of professing Christians at about 2 billion.

While "church" attendance seems to be increasing, it is not increasing as fast as the confusion surrounding the question of which is the right "church".

While it has been said, "They can't all be wrong", it is more correct to say, "They cannot all be right". If Christ built His EKKLESÍA as He said, then it can be found somewhere on Earth today —and it is the only right "church".

But we must ask: How do we find it? What do we look for? How do we identify it? How do we know it if we see it?

My mother required me to read many books when growing up. I enjoyed most of them and am thankful she did this.

On occasion, perhaps two or three times, I picked up the Bible and attempted to read it. However, I never got far, because it made no sense to me. I simply could not understand the Bible.

Despite this lack of understanding, upon turning ten, I was "baptized" into the "church" that I had been born into. I recall having to appear briefly before the "church" board, to answer several simple questions, which I no longer remember. I do recall making some kind of general affirmation about this denomination, but I also remember that I was not concerned in the least with whether or not I was in the right "church", or if I was fulfilling the Bible definition of a Christian.

Neither of these questions remotely interested me. I did vaguely believe that God existed, but He was not real to me. I had certainly never attempted to build a personal relationship with Him or find His true EKKLESÍA. I did not pray or study His Word for guidance or to learn about His principles.

Jesus said, "*But in vain they do worship Me, teaching as doctrines the precepts of men*" (**Matthew 15:9**). In Mark's parallel account of this statement, He continued, "*You are experts at setting aside the commandment of God in order to keep your tradition*" (7:9).

The world's Christianity is filled with traditions. One of the largest is the traditional view of the New Testament "church" (ekklesía). Most ministers, theologians, and religionists typically define the "church" in this way: "All those who sincerely believe in Jesus Christ as their Savior comprise the true "church". This is often followed with the familiar statement, "There are many routes to heaven" or "There are many spokes on the wheel of salvation".

Though the Bible does not teach that heaven is the reward of the saved, the clear implication of these statements is that people can believe what they want, or be a part of any group that they choose, and still be Christians. While people may sincerely believe these traditional ideas, they are sincerely WRONG.

The Bible declares, *"God is not God of confusion but of peace, as in all EKKLESÍAS of the saints* [citizens of the KINGDOM]" (1 Corinthians 14:33). The context shows this refers to all congregations of the true EKKLESÍA, not all organizations of men.

God's EKKLESÍA (composed of many congregations of citizens) was to reflect peace, not confusion. You do not need to be confused about the identity of the true EKKLESÍA.

God inspired Paul to write, *"But examine everything carefully; hold fast to that which is good"* (1 Thessalonians 5:21). While this obviously refers to scriptural matters (not what kind of car to drive or house to buy), it does say that "ALL things," not "some things", should be proven.

Surely God would not exclude something of such magnitude —such vital importance— as the matter of where His true EKKLESÍA is found. And He would never emphatically tell people to prove things that cannot be proven.

The more I have studied the Bible, the more I learned the religious "churches" of this world were wrong —on virtually everything. One scripture after another contradicted each traditional "church" theology I had been taught. I was amazed —actually stunned— at how easy it was to find direct, clear, undeniable proof that even the most popular traditions of the big denominations were not based on the Bible at all.

Each time I studied a Bible doctrine —salvation, baptism, who and what God is, the gospel, death, hell, law, sin, grace, being born again, the true origin of supposed "Christian" holidays, the sequence of prophetic events preceding Christ's Return, and so much more— I gained undeniable proof of what the Bible really taught.

I found that the religious "churches" of this world were almost invariably confused on all these and many other points of Bible teaching. The majority of "churches" and denominations were teaching a gospel that was not the gospel that Jesus preached nor that he commissioned the EKKLESÍA to preach. I discovered that the main emphasis of the gospel of today's "churches" evolves around going to heaven, and various dogmas of the different denominations.

When speaking to His disciples about the importance of seeking the Kingdom (government) of God, Jesus said, *"Do not be afraid, little flock, for your Father has chosen gladly to give you the Kingdom"* (**Luke 12:32**). By no stretch can "churches" comprised of millions, let alone a total of two billion, be considered a "little flock". Therefore, Christ's EKKLESÍA would not be readily visible.

Jesus understood that His EKKLESÍA —His little flock— would be persecuted and despised by the world. Just before His crucifixion, He warned, *"Remember the word that I said to you, 'A slave is not greater than his master.' If they persecuted Me, they will also persecute you; if they kept My word, they will keep yours also"* (**John 15:20**). In the previous verse, Jesus reminded His disciples *"I have chosen you out of the world, therefore the world hates you"*.

Jesus was persecuted, to the point of horrible crucifixion after a night of brutal torture. Therefore, the true EKKLESÍA could also expect to be persecuted —and hated.

Those in it are not "of the world". The world senses this and hates them for it (*"Because the mind set on the flesh is hostile toward God; for it does not subject itself to the law of God, for it is not even able to do so"*, **Romans 8:7**). Christ used Paul to record, *"Indeed, all who desire to live godly in Christ Jesus will be persecuted"* (**2 Timothy 3:12**).

The world's ecclesiastical "churches" have a host of different names, which are derived in various ways. These include the particular doctrines they teach, the names of the men who founded them, the humanly-devised type of "church" government that they espouse, their location, or their intended scope and size, such as universal or catholic, this latter to be thought of as all-encompassing.

On the night of His betrayal, Jesus prayed for His EKKLESÍA. Here is what He said:

> "[11]...Holy Father, keep through Your own name those whom You have given Me, that they may be one, as We are. [12] While I was with them in the world, I kept them in Your name [...] [14] I have given them Your word; and the world has hated them, because they are not of the world, even as I am not of the world. [15] I pray not that You should take them out of the world, but that You should keep them from the evil. [16] They are not of the world, even as I am not of the world. Sanctify them through Your truth: Your word is truth" John 17:11-12, 14-17

There are twelve separate places where the New Testament records that the true EKKLESÍA has been kept in the name of the Father God. Five refer to the entire EKKLESÍA, or body of Christ, as a whole. Another four speak of a specific local congregations, while using the same term "church of God". This may refer to the EKKLESÍA at Judea or Corinth, etc. Three other references speak collectively of all the individual local congregations combined. All these references use the term "churches" (ekklesías) of God" (Acts 20:28; 1 Cor. 1:2; 10:32; 11:16, 22; 15:9; 2 Cor. 1:1; Gal. 1:13; 1 Tim. 3:5, 15; 1 Thes. 2:14; 2 Thes. 1:4).

In the modern age, for corporate reasons, the "church" may use an additional descriptive name to distinguish itself from other "churches of God", those merely appropriating God's name, but not submitted to His government and obeying His commandments, believing His principles and truths or doing His Work.

Just as various mainstream denominations may have a few correct doctrines mixed with much error, some appropriate to themselves the name of God's "church".

Few "churches" may even have a significant amount of truth, but choose to accept a variety of false doctrines. We read how Jesus prayed in John 17, "*Sanctify them through Your truth: Your word is truth*".

The EKKLESÍA that Christ builds, directs, and guides it's sanctified —set apart— by its belief of the truth and principles of God's Word.

Men have their own differing definitions of what the "church" actually is, but only the Bible's definition—God's definition—matters. Read it for yourself "*...that you will know how one ought to conduct himself in the household of God, which is the EKKLESÍA of the living God, the pillar and support of the truth*" (**1 Timothy 3:15**). In the end, no other definition, devised by men, is acceptable. God's EKKLESÍA has and teaches the truth. The Eternal Gospel of The KINGDOM (government) of God.

We have discussed how this world's "churches" are in confusion, divided by endless disagreement over theology, doctrine and practice. Amos 3:3 ask, *"Do two men walk together unless they have made an appointment (agreement)?"* The answer is NO.

This world's "churches" do not practice the principle of *"Man shall not live by bread alone, but by every word of God"* (Luke 4:4), exactly as written. Instead, since they follow the many differing traditions of men, endless disagreements separate, divide, and create more and more "churches" of men. They generally do not "walk together", because they do not "agree"—either with each other or with God.

God's EKKLESÍA is different. Many New Testament verses show that the EKKLESÍA that Christ built is unified—with all its citizens and congregations walking together in complete agreement with each other, and with God and Christ.

An important point, demonstrating the unity of the true EKKLESÍA, emerges from Jesus's prayer in John 17, on the night of His betrayal. He prayed:

> "[19] For their sakes I sanctify Myself, that they themselves also may be sanctified in truth [...] through the truth... [21] that they may all be one; even as You, Father, *are* in Me and I in You, that they also may be in Us, so that the world may believe that You sent Me [22] The glory which You have given Me I have given to them, that they may be one, just as We are one; [23] I in them and You in Me, that they may be perfected in unity, so that the world may know that

You sent Me, and loved them, even as You have loved Me." John 17:19, 21-23

These are powerful statements. Jesus intended that His EKKLESÍA be unified—"one"—no less than were He and His Father. There is no room for disagreement in an EKKLESÍA that is this unified. These verses describe a perfect oneness through the truth—the same kind of oneness that the Father and Jesus enjoy.

It is this kind of unity that allows true Christians to be "in" them—be in Jesus and the Father (*"that they may all be one; even as You, Father, are in Me and I in You, that they also may be in Us, so that the world may believe that You sent Me"*, **John 17:21**). Even in the Old Testament, David was inspired to record, *"Behold, how good and how pleasant it is for brothers to dwell together in unity"* **(Psalms 133:1)**.

We now must examine several New Testament passages to see if, in fact, this kind of wonderful unity was apparent after the New Testament EKKLESÍA actually formed.

Did God's true servants teach and administer this kind of agreement? On the day of Pentecost, gathered in *"one accord"* **(Acts 2:1)**, when the New Testament EKKLESÍA came into existence, 3,000 converts were baptized. They formed the very beginning of Christ's building of His EKKLESÍA. The initial description given was *"They were continually devoting themselves to the apostles' teaching and to fellowship..."* **(Acts 2:42)**, *"...all those who had believed were together"* **(Acts 2:44)** and *"...they, Day by day continuing with one mind in the temple, and breaking bread from house to* *house, they were taking their meals together with gladness and sincerity of heart"* (Acts 2:46).

From these verses, we clearly see that the EKKLESÍA Christ built began in unity—agreement. —over doctrine, and together. Now verse 47: "*...And the Lord was adding to their number day by day those who were being saved"* (Acts 2:47). In the true EKKLESÍA, Jesus Christ guides and directs, He is the One who adds to it, building it.

Much can be learned by examining Paul's instructions to various congregations, he was overseeing. The Corinthian congregation had many problems—including terrible division and disunity. Paul strongly admonished them to stop entertaining other doctrines and to quit playing favorites with ministers. Notice:

> "[10] Now I exhort you, brethren, by the name of our Lord Jesus Christ, that you all agree and that there be no divisions among you, but that you be made complete in the same mind and in the same judgment. [...] [12] Now I mean this, that each one of you is saying, "I am of Paul," and "I of Apollos," and "I of Cephas," and "I of Christ." [13] Has Christ been divided? Paul was not crucified for you, was he? Or were you baptized in the name of Paul?" 1 Corinthians 1:10, 12-13

Do not miss the intent of this passage. Paul was inspired to describe, in five different ways, how completely all of God's people in every age should be unified and in agreement.

The Unknown Gospel

And these verses cannot be "spiritualized away" by deceptive human reasoning.

Later, in the same letter to Corinth, Paul recorded that the EKKLESÍA had many separate members (citizens), yet was like various parts of a human body, in that these members were connected.

> "¹² For even as the body is one and yet has many members, and all the members of the body, though they are many, are one body, so also is Christ. ¹³ For by one Spirit we were all baptized into one body, whether Jews or Greeks, whether slaves or free, and we were all made to drink of one Spirit. ¹⁴ For the body is not one member, but many." 1 Corinthians 12:12-14

The context uses the analogy of hands, feet, eyes, ears, and the mouth to show how different parts of a human body are connected within the same person. Paul continues: *"¹⁸ But now God has placed the members, each one of them, in the body, just as He desired. ¹⁹ If they were all one member, where would the body be? ²⁰ But now there are many members, but one body"* (1 Corinthians 12:18-20). These verses also cannot be "spiritualized away" by human reasoning. They do not describe an amorphous, disconnected; "spiritual" supposed "body" of disagreeing people and organizations throughout professing Christianity.

Any foot, eye, or ear that is taken from a human body dies. No severed body part can live for very long without blood supply and the connective tissue necessary to secure it to the body. God created the human body, so He obviously understands the analogy that He inspired.

Notice his statement to the Colossian congregation: *"And He [Christ] is also the head of the body, the "church" [ekklesía]"* (Colossians 1:18). The Bible definition of the body of Christ is the same as the EKKLESÍA. Paul admonished the Colossians to be *"knit together in love, and ... the full assurance of understanding"* and *"rooted and now being built up in Him and established in your faith, just as you were instructed..."* (Colossians 2:2 and 7). There is no misunderstanding the total unity Paul describes here. Brethren walk "together," assured of the right "understanding" that they "have been taught".

Now see his instruction to the Ephesians congregations. Speaking of what God placed under Christ's control, Paul wrote, "[22] *And He put all things in subjection under His feet, and gave Him [Christ] as Head over all things to the church [ekklesía], [23] which is His body, the fullnesss of Him who fills all in all"* (Ephesians 1:22-23). In chapter 4, Paul admonished the Ephesians:

> "[3] Being diligent to preserve the unity of the Spirit in the bond of peace. [4] There is one body [Ekklesía] and one Spirit, just as also you were called in one hope of your calling; [5] one Lord, one faith, one baptism, [6] one God and Father of all who is over all and through all and in all."
> Ephesians 4:3-6

Again, there must be no confusing the all-encompassing unity and agreement that this passage requires of God's people. Recall how Christ prayed for this kind of oneness and unity. A few verses later, Paul described the importance of a faithful ministry, actively working with and teaching Christ's EKKLESÍA. Carefully read and understand the following lengthy, important passage:

> "¹¹ And He gave some as apostles, and some as prophets, and some as evangelists, and some as pastors and teachers, ¹² for the equipping of the saints for the work of service, to the building up of the body of Christ; ¹³ until we all attain to the unity of the faith, and of the knowledge of the Son of God, to a mature man, to the measure of the stature which belongs to the fullness of Christ. ¹⁴ As a result, we are no longer to be children, tossed here and there by waves and carried about by every wind of doctrine, by the trickery of men, by craftiness in deceitful scheming; ¹⁵ but speaking the truth in love, we are to grow up in all aspects into Him who is the head, even Christ, ¹⁶ from whom the whole body, being fitted and held together by what every joint supplies, according to the proper working of each individual part, causes the growth of the body for the building up of itself in love." Ephesians 4:11-16

The EKKLESÍA is Christ's Body and, as its Head, He governs, directs, and builds it, adding to it daily. These verses describe it as being unified in both truth and love.

In phrase after phrase, this passage demonstrates that the entire "church" (*"whole body"* and *"every part"*) must be walking together in complete doctrinal agreement under Christ's authority. And He works through His true ministers to keep the EKKLESÍA from drifting into *"every wind of* [other] *doctrine."*

Now consider Paul's admonition to the Philippians congregation: *"...standing firm in one spirit, with one mind striving together for the faith of the gospel; 28 in no way alarmed by your opponents"* (Philippians 1:27-28). And, *"make my joy complete by being of the same mind, maintaining the same love, united in spirit, intent on one purpose"* (Philippians 2:2). These passages teach that complete unity in the EKKLESÍA is the only condition acceptable to God.

The local Roman congregations were experiencing a problem with false doctrines entering the "church" (ekklesía). Notice how Paul instructed them to address this:

> "[17] Now I urge you, brethren, keep your eye on those who cause dissensions and hindrances contrary to the teaching which you learned, and turn away from them. [18] For such men are slaves, not of our Lord Christ but of their own appetites; and by their smooth and flattering speech they deceive the hearts of the unsuspecting." Romans 16:17-18

This is strong language. However, it demonstrates how important it is to God that His people not stray from the truth into manmade teachings and traditions.

Peter also taught the all-important need for EKKLESÍA unity and oneness. He wrote, "*But you are a chosen race, a royal priesthood, a holy nation, a people for God's own possession, so that you may proclaim the excellencies of Him who has called you out of darkness into His marvelous light*" (1 Peter 2:9). The four phrases in this verse are in the singular — meaning one, not several, of each term referenced. For instance, if a nation is split into several nations, no one would consider it to be a single nation —it would be multiple nations, not "a" nation. The same is true of God's EKKLESÍA.

Jesus Himself taught this on the matter of ekklesía unity: "*Any kingdom divided against itself is laid waste; and any city or house divided against itself will not stand [survive]*" (Matthew 12:25). Paul asked in 1 Corinthians 1:13 ("*Has Christ been divided? Paul was not crucified for you, was he? Or were you baptized in the name of Paul?*"), "Is Christ divided?"

This is Christ's answer: His instruction is even more fascinating when the reader considers that He is describing Satan's kingdom in this account. Jesus taught that even the devil is smart enough to know that his kingdom cannot be divided and survive. Surely, the great God of heaven and Jesus Christ are at least as intelligent as Satan the devil. Of course, they are infinitely wiser. They both understand that their ekklesía also cannot be divided and expect to survive ("stand").

After the original apostles died, the great, false universal "church" did come in and largely destroy the visible EKKLESÍA.

Because of persecution, often including threats, imprisonment, torture and death, most people gave in and departed from the truth of God's Way and therefore from the true EKKLESÍA. This period is often called "The Lost Century". Yet, as Christ promised, His EKKLESÍA has always survived. It has never completely disappeared or been destroyed—though it has certainly remained a "little flock" that has kept His Word, and the EKKLESÍA that has always been kept in God's name.

Peter warned:

> "¹ But false prophets also arose among the people, just as there will also be false teachers among you, who will secretly introduce destructive heresies, even denying the Master who bought them, bringing swift destruction upon themselves. ² Many will follow their sensuality, and because of them the way of the truth will be maligned; ³ and in *their* greed they will exploit you with false words; their judgment from long ago is not idle, and their destruction is not asleep." 2 Peter 2:1-3

Before his death, Paul explicitly warned the Ephesians elders to understand what would happen after he was gone.

> "²⁸ Be on guard for yourselves and for all the flock, among which the Holy Spirit has made you overseers, to shepherd the "church" of God which He purchased with His own blood. ²⁹ I know that after my departure savage wolves will

come in among you, not sparing the flock; ³⁰ and from among your own selves men will arise, speaking perverse things, to draw away the disciples after them." (Acts 20:28-30

History records that this is exactly what happened during (and after) The Lost Century.

We read that Jesus promised that when false leaders, whom He refers to in John 10 as *"thieves and robbers"*, have been able to get into the fold, *"the sheep hear His [Christ's] voice: and He calls His own sheep by name, and leads them out"*. His voice is plainly defined in Scripture as *"the truth"* (*"Therefore Pilate said to Him, «So You are a king?» Jesus answered, «You say correctly that I am a king. For this I have been born, and for this I have come into the world, to testify to the truth. Everyone who is of the truth hears My voice»"*, John 18:37).

He went on in John 10 to add:

> "³ To him the doorkeeper opens, and the sheep hear his voice, and he calls his own sheep by name and leads them out. ⁴ When he puts forth all his own, he goes ahead of them, and the sheep follow him because they know his voice. ⁵ A stranger they simply will not follow, but will flee from him, because they do not know the voice of strangers." John 10:3-5

Christ continues by describing certain ministers: *"He flees because he is a hired hand and is not concerned about the sheep"* (John 10:13). This remarkable promise shows that Jesus will never abandon His sheep and will always protect those who hear His voice and willingly follow Him when they are in danger of false doctrines.

God's EKKLESÍA does not compromise on even one of His true doctrines. Just as Jesus foretold, it is a small, hated, and persecuted *"little flock"* that God has kept in His name. It is doing God's Work —taking the true gospel of the Kingdom (government) of God to the world before this age ends.

Its fruits are evidence of God's blessings. It is growing and has citizens scattered in countries around the world. God wants His sons to understand His purpose.

He has given a basic analogy that is easy to grasp. He compares His one ekklesía —His true EKKLESÍA— to the human body: *"^{12} For even as the body is one and yet has many members, and all the members of the body, though they are many, are one body, so also is Christ. ^{13} For by one Spirit we were all baptized into one body, whether Jews or Greeks, whether slaves or free, and we were all made to drink of one Spirit"* (1 Corinthians 12:12-13).

Colossians 1:18 and Ephesians 1:22-23 revealed that "body" means the EKKLESÍA.

There is only one ekklesía and, like the human body, all parts are connected. Head, eyes, ears, fingers, toes, arms, and legs are different but integrated parts of the human body. Paul added in chapter 12: *"^{27} Now you are Christ's body, and individually members of it. ^{28} And God has appoint-*

*ed in the "church" (*ekklesía*), first apostles, second prophets, third teachers..."* (1 Corinthians 12:27-28).

The EKKLESÍA is organized, structured —it has God's government. Throughout the New Testament, God depicts Himself as a Father with many "children" —those of His EKKLESÍA. Jesus continually referred to the other Person in the Godhead as "Father". He understood that He was a "Son" (*"¹ Paul, a bond-servant of Christ Jesus, called as an apostle, set apart for the gospel of God [...] ³ concerning His Son, who was born of a descendant of David according to the flesh"* Romans 1:1 and 3), has been resurrected from the dead, He has become a divine Son (*"who was declared the Son of God with power by the resurrection from the dead, according to the Spirit of holiness, Jesus Christ our Lord"*, Romans 1:4; *"But of the Son He says,'Your throne, O God, is forever and ever, and the righteous scepter is the scepter of His kingdom"*, Hebrews 1:8). Carefully read Romans 1:1-4 to see that Christ was, in fact, a descendant of David —a fleshly human— through His mother:

> "¹ Paul, a bond-servant of Christ Jesus, called *as* an apostle, set apart for the gospel of God, ² which He promised beforehand through His prophets in the holy Scriptures, ³ concerning His Son, who was born of a descendant of David according to the flesh, ⁴ who was declared the Son of God with power by the resurrection from the dead, according to the Spirit of holiness, Jesus Christ our Lord."

Christ had a human mother, Mary. He has a Spirit Father (of course, Joseph was not His actual father). Think for a moment. God sired Jesus in the womb of a human woman. This is an extraordinary statement to understand. Grasp what it means: The God kind (the Father) reproduces like any other kind. God selected a virgin human (one made in *"His form and likeness"*) to bear His Son. Yet, this was not in any sense "improper", because God was not reproducing outside of His own kind.

Remember, God ordained that all animals and humans—all living things—reproduce after *"his kind"* (*"God made the beasts of the earth after their kind, and the cattle after their kind, and everything that creeps on the ground after its kind; and God saw that it was good"*, **Genesis 1:25**). The Father's (spirit) begettal of Jesus in a (physical) human defies any other explanation.

After His death and Resurrection, and return to being Spirit, Christ became the *"firstborn* [Son] *from the dead"* (**Colossians 1:18**). He experienced a second birth into the Family of God by a Resurrection. Romans 1:4 says that Christ was *"the Son of God...by the resurrection from the dead"*. This is what made Christ a Son. And it represents how human beings are saved.

Many verses show that Christ is God. He is a divine Son, a member of the divine God Family. Hebrews 1:8 makes this clear. There, the Father refers to His Son —Christ— as God. *"Your throne, O God* [Christ], *is forever and ever"* (**Hebrew 1:8**). Grasp these verses. Christ is a born Son by resurrection from the dead.

Let us tie this understanding directly to the EKKLESÍA.

What is the final destiny of the EKKLESÍA? Exactly what happens immediately after the resurrection of the dead? The answer is staggering. First, we must define exactly who and what the CITIZENS of the EKKLESÍA are.

Return to Romans 8 and now read verse 9: *"However, you are not in the flesh but in the Spirit, if indeed the Spirit of God dwells in you. But if anyone does not have the Spirit of Christ, he does not belong to Him"*.
To be a Christian, one must have the Spirit of God. It is that simple.

Recall that 1 Corinthians 12:13 revealed that all members of the ekklesía are "baptized into one body." Baptized means immersed, put into. Therefore, a Christian is put into God's ekklesía by receiving the Holy Spirit. This Spirit makes him a begotten son (*"and if children, heirs also, heirs of God and fellow heirs with Christ, if indeed we suffer with Him so that we may also be glorified with Him"*, **Romans 8:17**). Those without God's Spirit, regardless of their "church" affiliation or denomination, are "none of His".

However, there is more important knowledge to understand. It is tied directly to the purpose for human marriage and family. The way a husband loves, works with, and leads his wife is intended to be a reflection of Christ's leadership over His ekklesía.

The New Testament actually identifies the EKKLESÍA as Christ's betrothed Bride: *"For I am jealous for you with a godly jealousy; for I betrothed you to one husband, so that to Christ I might present you as a pure virgin"* (2 Corinthians 11:2).

First, notice the following parallel between Christ and His EKKLESÍA, and human husbands and their wives:

> "²³ For the husband is the head of the wife, as Christ also is the head of the church (ekklesía), He Himself *being* the Savior of the body [...] ²⁷ that He might present to Himself the church (ekklesía) in all her glory, having no spot or wrinkle or any such thing; but that she would be holy and blameless." Ephesians 5:23, 27

The Bible reveals that the converted husband's relationship with his wife is a parallel of Christ's relationship to the EKKLESÍA.

Christ works with His ekklesía the way husbands are to work with their wives. He intends to *"present it* [the ekklesía] *to Himself"*, in a marriage ceremony, with all spots, wrinkles, and blemishes gone. However, this wedding is only attainable for those learning the lessons of this life —those who gain experience through suffering and building character now.

> "¹¹ And I saw heaven opened, and behold, a white horse, and He who sat on it is called Faithful and True, and in righteousness He judges and wages war. ¹² His eyes are a flame of fire, and on His head are many diadems; and

The Unknown Gospel

> He has a name written on Him which no one knows except Himself. [13] He is clothed with a robe dipped in blood, and His name is called The Word of God. [14] And the armies which are in heaven, clothed in fine linen, white and clean, were following Him on white horses. [15] From His mouth comes a sharp sword, so that with it He may strike down the nations, and He will rule them with a rod of iron; and He treads the wine press of the fierce wrath of God, the Almighty. [16] And on His robe and on His thigh He has a name written, KING OF KINGS, AND LORD OF LORDS." Revelation 19:11-16

After Christ returns and re-establishes the government of God, He becomes Ruler and Governor over all nations on Earth, with His ekklesía. *"Then the seventh angel sounded; and there were loud voices in heaven, saying,"The kingdom of the world has become the kingdom of our Lord and of His Christ; and He will reign forever and ever"* (Revelation 11:15). However, this is not all. Immediately, upon His Return, here is what Christ does:

> "[6] Then I heard something like the voice of a great multitude and like the sound of many waters and like the sound of mighty peals of thunder, saying,"Hallelujah. For the Lord our God, the Almighty, reigns. [7] Let us rejoice and be glad and give the glory to Him, for the marriage of the Lamb has come and His bride has made herself ready." [8] It was given to her to clothe

> herself in fine linen, bright and clean; for the fine linen is the righteous acts of the saints. ⁹Then he *said to me, "Write, 'Blessed are those who are invited to the marriage supper of the Lamb…" Revelation 19:6-9

Of course, the Lamb of God has always been Jesus Christ ("²⁹*The next day he saw Jesus coming to him and said, "Behold, the Lamb of God who takes away the sin of the world* […] ³⁶ *and he looked at Jesus as He walked, and said, "Behold, the Lamb of God!"* John 1:29, 36).

Now fully comprehend this awesome knowledge: Christ is God. He is of the "God kind". Just as God and Christ could not reproduce outside their kind anymore than any animal could reproduce with any other kind, Christ could not marry outside the God kind either.

> "²⁴Then God said, "Let the earth bring forth living creatures after their kind: cattle and creeping things and beasts of the earth after their kind"; and it was so. ²⁵ God made the beasts of the earth after their kind, and the cattle after their kind, and everything that creeps on the ground after its kind; and God saw that it was good. ²⁶Then God said, "Let Us make man in Our image, according to Our likeness; and let them rule over the fish of the sea and over the birds of the sky and over the cattle and over all the earth, and over every creeping thing that creeps on the earth." Genesis 1:24-26

At His Return, in one of the most awesome events in all history, Christ will marry His ekklesía. This is the truth from God's Word —and you have just seen it.

The Old Covenant agreement between Jesus and ancient Israel was actually a marriage agreement, or covenant. In Jeremiah 3:14 (KJV), God said to Israel, *"I am married unto you"*. Though He did later divorce her (Jeremiah 3:8) for unfaithfulness, the marriage remained binding until Jesus's death.

Jesus's marriage to, and divorce from, ancient Israel followed Old Testament law —see Ezekiel 16:38 and Deuteronomy 24:1. Now understand again that ancient Israel was actually the Old Testament "church". Many places in the Old Testament refers to her as the "congregation of Israel". Acts 7:38 refers to Israel as the "congregation in the wilderness".

The New Testament is different; in that it involves spiritual promises, **having to do with grace, not merely race**. However, Gentiles (those of other races) were permitted to become part of ancient Israel, but only on the condition that they kept the laws, statutes, and judgments that governed the country.

All marriages end when either spouse dies. In the case of ancient Israel, her marriage ended —was no longer binding— because Jesus, through His sacrifice, died. After His Resurrection, Jesuschrist was now free —eligible— to remarry. The New Testament EKKLESÍA today is still Israel, only she is spiritual, not physical, in nature. She is also not confined to a particular race of people.

Here is what Paul wrote to the Ephesians congregation, which was almost entirely Gentile:

> "¹¹ Therefore remember that formerly you, the Gentiles in the flesh, who are called "Uncircumcision" by the so-called "Circumcision," which is performed in the flesh by human hands— ¹² remember that you were at that time separate from Christ, excluded from the commonwealth of Israel, and strangers to the covenants of promise, having no hope and without God in the world. ¹³ But now in Christ Jesus you who formerly were far off have been brought near by the blood of Christ.[...] ¹⁹ So then you are no longer strangers and aliens, but you are fellow citizens with the saints, and are of God's household." Ephesians 2:11-13, 19

Christ's sacrifice was for the whole world (*"For God so loved the world, that He gave His only begotten Son, that whoever believes in Him shall not perish, but have eternal life"*, John 3:16). This includes Gentiles, who are the vast, predominant number of people on Earth.

Most physical Israelites are, at this time, and with the world, cut off from God by sin. They are not yet included in spiritual Israel —the EKKLESÍA.

The Unknown Gospel

The Gentile Galatians also understood that they were included within spiritual Israel. Notice: *"And if you be Christ's, then you are* [the Gentile Galatians] Abraham's descendants [Israel], heirs according to promise" (Galatians 3:29). The Galatians were part of spiritual Israel by grace, not race. Romans 11, particularly verses 25-26, explains this in detail:

> "^{25} For I do not want you, brethren, to be uninformed of this mystery—so that you will not be wise in your own estimation—that a partial hardening has happened to Israel until the fullness of the Gentiles has come in; ^{26} and so all Israel will be saved; just as it is written,"The Deliverer will come from Zion, He will remove ungodliness from Jacob."

We have seen that the entire ekklesía is to marry Christ at His Return and the establishing of the Kingdom of God. Matthew 22 shows this: *"The kingdom of heaven may be compared to a king who gave a wedding feast for his son"* (v. 2). God is the "King" and Christ is the "Son" in this parable.

Matthew 25 also describes this coming marriage:

> "^{1}Then the kingdom of heaven will be comparable to ten virgins, who took their lamps and went out to meet the bridegroom […] ^{6} But at midnight there was a shout, 'Behold, the bridegroom. Come out to meet him…[…] ^{10} And while they were going away to make the pur-

> chase, the bridegroom came, and those who were ready went in with him to the wedding feast; and the door was shut." Matthew 25:1, 6, 10

The door "was shut" because some will be kept out. There will be many today who will be terribly disappointed because their ignorance of God's Plan will (temporarily for some, permanently for others) excludes them from being part of the bride.

The state of marriage in the world today is in confusion. Many choose to live together prior to marriage, or are rejecting this God-ordained institution altogether. Others are pursuing same-sex marriage, or other "alternative lifestyles". All these completely miss the divinely revealed supreme purpose of marriage —what it is intended to picture.

Certainly, no one who rejects the great transcendent meaning and overarching purpose of marriage will ever be permitted to be part of the bride that marries Christ. That would mock God's purpose and reward rebellion.

God calls His EKKLESÍA, His future Bride, "a building" that is "being fitted together" (Ephesians 2:21). Christ is literally *"building a building"* consisting of *"living stones"* (1 Peter 2:5). Psalm 127:1 declares, *"Unless the Lord builds the house, They labor in vain who build it; Unless the Lord guards the city, The watchman keeps awake in vain..."* (we saw that 1 Timothy 3:15 calls God's ekklesía *"the house of God"*). Christ is continuing His building of the ekklesía today, and you have come in contact with it.

We have seen that the true ekklesía is also pictured as a bride prophesied to marry Jesus Christ at His Return:

> "⁷Let us rejoice and be glad and give the glory to Him, for the marriage of the Lamb has come and His bride has made herself ready. ⁸It was given to her to clothe herself in fine linen, bright and clean; for the fine linen is the righteous acts of the saints. ⁹Then he said to me, 'Write, Blessed are those who are invited to the marriage supper of the Lamb' And he said to me, 'These are true words of God'."
> Revelation 19:7-9

She is described as, at that time, having "made herself ready" for this wonderful and glorious event.

Finally, we have not yet addressed the actual meaning of the Greek word translated "church" in the New Testament.

This needs clarification. Most have supposed it means a building or an organization, when it means neither. The word "church" is ekklesía, meaning "a calling out," especially as a religious congregation. Christians are indeed called out of this world —its ways, its customs, its practices, its traditions, its false knowledge— and into the true EKKLESÍA, and fellowship with God and Christ (1 John 1:3). Take time to savor this marvelous understanding, we cover this in chapter 5 and 6.

God thunders this to all people everywhere:

> "¹⁷ But the one who joins himself to the Lord is one spirit with Him. ¹⁸ Flee immorality. Every other sin that a man commits is outside the body, but the immoral man sins against his own body." 2 Corinthians 6:17-18

May God help you to come out of the Babylon of this world (*"I heard another voice from heaven, saying, Come out of her, my people, so that you will not participate in her sins and receive of her plagues"*, **Revelation 18:4**), that you may qualify to rule with the all-powerful, living Christ in the wonderful, new world that lies ahead.

Some few are choosing to come out of the world. They are willing to seek God with all their hearts. These are those called of God at this time. Let us understand. Most professing Christians have been taught that God is trying to save the world now. This thinking goes something like this: God and the devil are at war over the fate of mankind. This is seen as a desperate struggle between good and evil — God and Satan. We saw that Revelation 12:9 states that Satan has deceived the whole world —and the picture of how God will eventually save all mankind is his greatest deception.

Of course, this picture serves Satan, because he would love to have the world think that he is more powerful than God.

When speaking of Christ's name, the Bible says, *"And there is salvation in no one else; for there is no other name under heaven that has been given among men by which we must be saved"* (Acts 4:12). Further, Romans 10:13 states that men must call on this name to be saved.

It is obvious that all who have not yielded to the God of the Bible and accepted Jesus Christ, as their Savior and Lord are certainly not saved. Countless billions have died in this condition. Most have assumed that the only other option for these is that they were lost to salvation and that God long ago planned this for the vast majority who has ever lived.

Again, if the war is to almost feverishly "win souls for Christ", as most supposed Christian ministers depict it, then the devil is much stronger, and much more effective, in his effort than God is.

This is the only other possibility —unless there is a third category containing the vast majority of people. However, it must be a category that has not been recognized.
The truth is that God is carefully calling out of the deceived masses to understand His eternal Plan and the true principles of the Bible.

The very definition of what is the New Testament EKKLESÍA forces an examination of the subject of being "called". What does it mean to be "called"?

Many naturally wonder if God is calling them. How can one know? Are feelings sufficient on such a vital matter? What is a calling? What does God's Word say?

The Bible does speak of those who have been called by God. Notice what Paul said to the Thessalonian brethren: *"Faithful is He [God] that calls you, and He also will bring it to pass"* (1 Thessalonians 5:24).

As a warning to the Galatians congregation, who were losing sight of the true gospel, he said this: *"I am amazed that you are so quickly deserting Him who called you by the grace of Christ, for a different gospel"* (Galatians 1:6), and later added, *"⁷ You were running well; who hindered you from obeying the truth? ⁸ This persuasion did not come from Him who calls you"* (Galatians 5:7-8).

To the Corinthian congregation he wrote, *"For consider your calling, brethren, that there were not many wise according to the flesh, not many mighty, not many noble"* (1 Corinthians 1:26).

Jesus Himself spoke on many occasions about the Christian calling. You may be familiar with His statement, *"For many are called, but few are chosen"* (Matthew 22:14 and 20:16). Later, adding meaning to the second part of this phrase, He explained this to His disciples: *"You did not choose Me but I chose you"* (John 15:16), and then *"but I chose you out of the world, because of this the world hates you"* (John 15:19).

When placed together, these passages explain that God is calling a people out of the world for His supreme purpose. Those who respond to His calling are then "chosen", going on to repentance, baptism, and conversion.

Over time, many find themselves learning things that they have never heard before. They discover that there is a correct (a true) understanding of the Bible's principles and truths, and there is a wrong one. They come to recognize that they have been brought into contact with extraordinary understanding, unknown to all around them. They notice that the Bible makes sense —which it is not as hard to understand as they had previously thought.

Then, feeling a growing need to act on what they are learning, many wonder, "Am I being called by God?" Sometimes this question takes the form of "Am I undergoing 'conversion'?" or "Should I get baptized?" or even "Have I come in contact with God's true "church" (ekklesía)?" At best, most are unsure of how to answer these basic questions, and many have absolutely no idea whatsoever how to even properly address them.

Let us see from God's Word, how to know if God is calling you. It can be made simple, virtually impossible to misunderstand. After all, this question is one of the most important you will ever face. Properly understanding its answer is of paramount importance to your life.

I first began learning God's truth when I was 39 years old. Before God called me, I had not known the principles and truths of the Bible. I remember being astonished at how clear the Bible became —and how exciting it was to study. Prior to this —throughout the time I attended the well-known, respected denomination of my youth— I had always found the Bible boring and hard to understand.

People of all ages and backgrounds puzzle over just what a "calling" is. Many reduce it to little more than a particular feeling that comes over them, which they attribute to God.

Millions in the world feel "called" —in some cases to the "church", in other cases to the "ministry", or "missionary work", in still other cases to work with children, and in yet others to serve in the medical profession or even in the military.

Ignorant of what God says, so many people are left to rely on mere feelings, assuming that their lives —and the paths they choose— are divinely inspired. They attribute this "inspiration" to being called of God. Sadly, most never learn that these "callings" have nothing to do with following the true God of the Bible.

A true calling from God is much more than a kind of abstract feeling that human reasoning is only too happy to conclude is "from God". Jesus stated, *"No one can come to Me unless the Father who sent Me draws him…"* (John 6:44). Nineteen verses later, He repeated to His audience, *"For this reason I have said to you, that no one can come to Me unless it has been granted him from the Father"* (John 6:65).

In the next verse, John records that *"As a result of this many of His disciples withdrew and were not walking with Him anymore"* (John 6:66).

Many who heard Jesus's statements simply could not understand that God has to "draw" people and that a calling is something that is "given" to them.

While many today appear to understand that they must in some fashion be called, they do not seek to understand from the Bible, how to know for certain that it is God who is calling –drawing– giving to them whatever it is they are to receive.

In Matthew, the disciples asked, *"Why speak you to them [the multitudes who heard Him] in parables?"* (Matthew 13:10). His answer summarizes how and with what God calls: *"Jesus answered them, 'To you it has been granted to know the mysteries of the kingdom of heaven, but to them it has not been granted'"* (Matthew 13:11). The next several verses amplify what He meant, explaining how many in the world can hear the truths of God (the "mysteries of the Kingdom –government–") but not grasp them.

Since the overwhelming majority of mankind is not being drawn by the power of God's Spirit, they have not been given the ability to comprehend God's Word.

How does this apply to you? The answer directly explains how to know if God is calling you: a calling, in the simplest terms, is understand the truths of God when you see, read, or hear them. Ask yourself: «Do I understand Bible teachings and truths when I hear them? Do the scriptures about the gospel of the Kingdom (government) of God; the plan of salvation and the purpose of human existence; God's warning message to His people; His Law; the Holy Days; tithing; the principles that the constitution of His Government has for every citizen of his holy nation; the one true EKKLESÍA; and many other teachings make sense to me?»

When you read or hear these things do they have meaning to you? Are you grasping them? Are they clear to your understanding? Do you see them as special knowledge others do not have? Do you feel tempted to pinch yourself in disbelief that you could be shown things of which the masses have no idea?

If the answers to these questions are "yes", then God is calling (drawing) you. The mysteries of the Kingdom (government) of God are being given to you.

Babies are born knowing nothing. They do not know even the basics of right and wrong. They have to be taught virtually everything. Similarly, the world does not know the things of God —spiritual right from spiritual wrong. However, with the knowledge of these things comes the responsibility to act on them.

Two Bible passages demonstrate that God holds people accountable for what they understand. James 4:17: *"Therefore, to one who knows the right thing to do and does not do it, to him it is sin"*. Now read Hebrews 10:26: *"For if we go on sinning willfully after receiving the knowledge of the truth, there no longer remains a sacrifice for sins"*.

Each time you learn more of God's truth (what is "good"), and it makes sense to you —you at least generally understand it— you are being given extraordinary spiritual knowledge for which God holds you accountable.

Comprehending —grasping the meaning of— knowledge is central to the calling process.

Further, seeing that you are being given special knowledge makes understanding how God calls one much more serious than most have believed.

Therefore, you are responsible now for the knowledge that you are being given. If one does not act on what he is learning, God will take that understanding away (*"for it is not the hearers of the Law who are just before God, but the doers of the Law will be justified"*, **Romans 2:13**; *"The fear of the Lord is the beginning of wisdom; A good understanding have all those who do His commandments; His praise endures forever"*, **Psalms 111:10**), and such a person is in a grave spiritual condition.

God's truth is most exciting to understand. It is the path to all the wonderful, good things in life—things God wants you to have. It is also the path to the greatest freedom that there is.

Jesus told certain Jews professing to believe on Him: *"If you continue in My word* [**the truth – John 17:17**], *then you are truly disciples of Mine; 32 and you will know the truth, and the truth will make you free"* (**John 8:31-32**). You must be willing to "continue" in your studies of God's Word, learning ever more of His truth, which Jesus explains will "make you free" from a world cut off from God and held captive by Satan. Even this understanding is precious knowledge.

Your associates in the world probably understand none of these things. Neither do your relatives. Without God's calling, they have no possible way of enjoying now what is being offered to you —if you are understanding and acting upon God's truth. It is also vital that you make certain in your mind the things you are learning. You should find yourself wanting to prove the doctrines of God. Paul also told the Thessalonians to *"But examine everything carefully; hold fast to that which is good"* (1 Thessalonians 5:21).

When you are unclear on a matter, remember that Jesus taught, *"Ask, and it will be given to you; seek, and you will find; knock, and it will be opened to you"* (Matthew 7:7).

Jesus said, when speaking to His disciples about the Holy Spirit they were soon to receive: *"that is the Spirit of truth, whom the world cannot receive, because it does not see Him or know Him, but you know Him because He abides with you and will be in you"* (John 14:17).

At this point, the disciples were much like many today — perhaps like you, too. They were seeing many spiritual truths in part, but did not yet fully grasp the enormous importance of learning God's Plan and way of life. Through the Holy Spirit working with them, God was revealing certain things that they would only understand in a greater way once it was in them, beginning at conversion. Ultimately, to fully understand all the things of God —all the mysteries of the Kingdom of God— one must be begotten of the Holy Spirit.

Satan is a master deceiver. He has proliferated many forms of false religions all over the earth. He counterfeits the truth in endless ways, and God's calling process is no exception.

CHAPTER 4
♦♦♦

WHAT IS THE CHURCH?

> "⁹ For we are God's fellow workers; you are God's field, God's building [...] ¹⁶ Do you not know that you are a temple of God and that the Spirit of God dwells in you?"
> 1 Corinthians 3:9 and 16

I understand that as times change, many terms change in meaning, but for the sake of biblical orthodoxy, one of my pet peeves has GOT to be when believers call a building or a place on a map a "church".

The "church", more specifically, the ekklesía, is defined in the bible as a people.

The ekklesía Christ is building is his own literal body. Every believer in Christ is part of Christ's ekklesía, and you will NEVER see in the bible where the "church" was ever referred to as a building or a place on a map...NEVER.

The ekklesía Christ is building is a living breathing organism where Christ is literally and prominently the Head.

The stones, which make this body, are living stones…you and me. *"You also, as living stones, are being built up as a spiritual house for a holy priesthood, to offer up spiritual sacrifices acceptable to God through Jesus Christ"* (**1 Peter 2:5**).

The book of Revelation describes different gatherings of the ekklesía or "churches" in those cities in Asia Minor. Many epistles are named after the cities where the ekklesía in those cities is being addressed.

Do you know what you're saying when you say "we are-going to church"? Certainly, we know what you mean…indeed…you might mean that you are going to a building where you get your religion done every week. You might be referring to the ritualistic custom and tradition of going to a building made with a steeple on top to worship.

It may mean a lot of things today of which I can't seem to find in the scriptures. If you asked your average Christian «what is the "church"?» you would probably be pointed to a place of worship (building). They might even invite you to their "church".

There is a paradigm here that MUST shift. Many give lip service to the real definition of the "church"; yet in their actions deny that truth by calling the building they attend as "the church".

God has many promises, warnings, rebukes, encouragement, etc. for His ekklesía through His word. *"**The God** *who made the world and all things in it, since He is Lord of heaven and earth, does not dwell in temples made with hands"* (Acts 17:24). When you call "church" the building that you attend, then you are NOT talking about the ekklesía Christ is building, but the "church" man has built.

Lets take the example of Paul (Saul): *"But Saul began ravaging the church* [ekklesía], *entering house after house, and dragging off men and women, he would put them in prison"* (Acts 8:3).

When Saul had his encounter with the Lord, Christ was very specific in letting him know whom he was persecuting. Note that it was not a building or any physical structure or human institution:

> "¹Now Saul, still breathing threats and murder against the disciples of the Lord, went to the high priest, ²and asked for letters from him to the synagogues at Damascus, so that if he found any belonging to the Way, both men and women, he might bring them bound to Jerusalem. ³As he was traveling, it happened that he was approaching Damascus, and suddenly a light from heaven flashed around him; ⁴and he fell to the ground and heard a voice saying to him, "Saul, Saul, why are you persecuting Me?" ⁵And he said, "Who are You, Lord?" And He said, "I am Jesus whom you are persecuting, ⁶but get up and enter the city, and it will be told you what you must do." Acts 9:1-6

It was HIM, his literal body. Saul was persecuting His PEOPLE. Confusing a locale on a street with the ekklesía Christ is building takes away the biblical significance of the purpose of the ekklesía.

The body of Christ is stuck today in an Old Testament mindset concerning the temple of God, which ultimately results in a works oriented system of bondage over the people of God.

The Jews went to offer sacrifices in their physical temple in Jerusalem, but lest not forget, that Jesus has taken away that system and priesthood out of existence with his sacrifice on the cross.

> "[9] When He said, «Behold, I have come to do Your will.» He takes away the first in order to establish the second." Hebrews 10:9
> "[12] For when the priesthood is changed, of necessity there takes place a change of law also." Hebrew 7:12

We treat the "church" building as a literal temple, as a place where God "dwells" and is "invited" in an invocation, where there is an "altar" for Christians to pray, and a pulpit where only the select cast of "high priests" who mediate on our behalf sit exalted over the body. Why they are trying to "resurrect" a temple God will no longer dwell in is beyond my understanding.

Christ, would have us be His ekklesía, and abide in Him. If we do that as a body, we are dangerous to the kingdom of darkness. We will go into the entire world and preach the Gospel of the Kingdom (government) of Heaven.

We will feed the hungry, visit the sick, take care of orphans, and maybe even raise some from the dead.

The ekklesía in the book of Acts was a vibrant ekklesía who was constantly in action, rarely stagnant, never tied down to a location, and always growing, letting the "acts" of the Holy Spirit be manifest before men.

As a result, God added to his ekklesía daily. This is how people will know that God is with us…it is through the power of the Gospel of the Kingdom, and the affect the Kingdom has on the lives of those who believe and have been changed by it. We can no longer be stagnant as a body and leave all of our godly gifts inside a building.

The true ekklesía is a nation of citizens that are having a daily effect in its communities where they are living. Not a physical structure on some street where religious activities take place from week to week.

> **"Unless the Lord builds the house, They labor in vain who build it; Unless the Lord guards the city, The watchman keeps awake in vain."**
> **Psalms 127:1**

CHAPTER 5
♦ ♦ ♦

EKKLESÍA VS. CHURCH

> "I also say to you that you are Peter, and upon this rock I will build My "church"; and the gates of Hades will not overpower it."
> Matthew 16:18

In Greek culture, *ekklesía* [ἐκκλησία] was the governing body that influenced and established the government in cities, regions and nations. It was an assembly in Athenian democracy (Ancient Greece). The Athenian reformer, legislator, statesman and poet Solon established it in 594 BC. This assembly was popular in those days since all citizens older than 20 years regardless of class, could belong to it.

The Ekklesía was used to nominate judges who were appointed by vote. They would also elect indirectly the components of the Areopagus (Judges of the High Court), who were chosen by the magistrate's selected by the Ekklesía.

The assembly (ekklesía) had the last word in:

- The Athenian law
- Declarations of war
- The signing of peace treaties
- The military strategy
- The choice of Strategos (General of the Greek militia)
- It had the ability to call the magistrate's to accountability at the end of each year in office

In classical Greek, *ekklesía* means 'assembly of citizens summoned by the herald or messenger of the legislative assembly'.

Solon, reformed the Athenian law and hence was born the Ekklesía, as a solution to corruption and injustice on the part of the rich and the rulers.

The Ekklesía was born to alleviate the condition of the peasants surrounded by poverty, debt, slavery and oppressed by the ruling lords:

> "[1] *The Spirit of the Lord God is upon me, Because the Lord has anointed me To bring good news to the afflicted; He has sent me to bind up the brokenhearted, To proclaim liberty to captives And freedom to prisoners;* [2] *To proclaim the favorable year of the Lord And the day of vengeance of our God; To comfort all who mourn.*" Isaiah 61: 1-2

It was an assembly made up of citizens that were called from outside the Civil Government and originally did not recieve a salary.

The word *ekklesía* also contains the definition 'People called for a cause or purpose '.

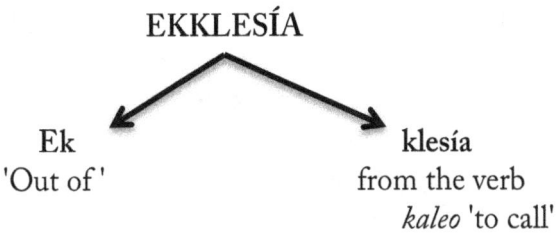

EKKLESÍA

Ek
'Out of '

klesía
from the verb
kaleo 'to call'

The 'called out' were people convened from outside the government system, to contribute to the supervision thereof and help in containing corruption.

Jesus said in Matthew 16:18 *"I will build my ekklesía..."*. In Greek culture an ekklesía was the ruling body that governed the nations, regions and cities. Thus Jesus didn't create a new word but borrowed from a common political word to describe His goal for those who would be His disciples; that they would represent His Kingdom (government) on earth with binding and loosing powers, that would govern the heavenly principalities and thus transform earthly communities where each ekklesía was established with His Kingdom (government).

> "I will give you the keys of the kingdom of heaven; and whatever you bind on earth shall have been bound in heaven, and whatever you loose on earth shall have been loosed in heaven." Matthew 16:19

> "So that the manifold wisdom of God might now be made known through the church to the rulers and the authorities in the heavenly places." Ephesians 3:10
>
> "For our struggle is not against flesh and blood, but against the rulers, against the powers, against the world forces of this darkness, against the spiritual forces of wickedness in the heavenly places." Ephesians 6:12

Once the ekklesía is built by Christ *"the GATES* [authority] *of Hades would not prevail against it"* (Matthew 16:20). This is a big difference in function from the typical "church" or congregation today whose primary purpose is to congregate and have weekly meetings.

The idea of conversion was not merely meant to fill seats for "church" growth, but to nurture disciples who would turn the world order upside down (*"When they did not find them, they began dragging Jason and some brethren before the city authorities, shouting, These men who have upset the world have come here also"*, Acts 17:6).

Since the late 19th century the idea of "church" as a ruling ekklesía has largely been lost and replaced with rescuing sinners from this world and living secluded pietistic lives to make it to heaven.

This is totally contrary to the original Greek meaning of the word ekklesía, which means being called to engage the world and govern it.

The Unknown Gospel

Pastors are happy to have a lot of people show up on Sundays, whether they affect the culture or not.

> **We went from changing the world to resisting the world, from engaging the world to protecting ourselves from the world.**

"Church" attendance in this nation is at an all-time high but cultural effectiveness is at an all-time low.

If the ekklesía is going to recapture its cultural commission of discipling nations and having global influence, as found in Genesis 1:28 ("*God blessed them; and God said to them, «Be fruitful and multiply, and fill the earth, and subdue it; and rule over the fish of the sea and over the birds of the sky and over every living thing that moves on the earth»*") and Matthew 28:19 ("*Go therefore and make disciples of all the nations, baptizing them in the name of the Father and the Son and the Holy Spirit*"), it has to learn the difference between building an ekklesía and a mere congregation that assembles together.

God has had to raise up some "para-church" ministries that function more like "special forces" with a call to reach cities. It may not be a pure New Testament model, but until local "churches" stop being inwardly focused and effectively reach their cities, God will continue to call "special forces" out of its ranks.

Sometimes a smaller-sized ekklesía can have more cultural influence than a "mega-church" that compromises the gospel of the Kingdom. Many of today's "mega-churches" are not ekklesías but are merely gathering places that have very limited influence in the heavenly and earthly realms.

Furthermore, this also explains why some "churches" experience more strategic-level spiritual warfare and others don't; mere congregations have lower-level spiritual warfare than those that function as the ekklesías of communities.

The following are some of the contrasts between the traditional "church" and the ekklesía that Christ wants to build:

EKKLESÍA	CHURCH
Challenges the status quo.	Assembles to find peace in the midst of the cultural environment
Demands a commitment that involves the vocational calling of all its members to represent the Kingdom (government) in all of life.	Demands a commitment that involves Sunday ministry and "church" programs.
Trains people for all of life.	Trains people for "church" or denominational life.
Effects change in the surrounding community.	Only affects change in its individual members.
Is at war against demonic entities in the heavenly spheres.	Is at war to have "church" growth and bring deliverance to some individual members.

EKKLESÍA	CHURCH
Sends out people to serve their communities.	Gathers from their communities to attend their various weekly meetings.
Is only satisfied with bringing the Kingdom (government) on earth.	Is satisfied if their members have joy in their hearts.
Expands Kingdom (government) influence by converting people to become AMBASSADORS for Christ.	Appeals to the felt needs of people so they will continually depend on a 60-90 minute Sunday worship experience to feel good about themselves.
Is outwardly focused on stewarding the earth.	Is focused on making it to heaven.
Engages in Spirit-empowered humanitarianism.	Engages on Spirit-empowered pietism.
Those in an ekklesía know they have been sanctified to serve others.	Those in a congregation believe they are saved for the sake of sanctification.
Teaches God's sovereign purpose for the saints since their physical birth (Ephesians 1:4-12, 2:10, Romans 8:28-30).	Only honors what God has done in saints spiritually from the time they were "born again".
Preaches Jesus rose from the dead to "fill all things" and "be all in all" (Ephesians 4:10, 1 Corinthians 15:28).	Preaches Jesus rose from the dead merely to save individuals from hell and take them to heaven.

EKKLESÍA	CHURCH
Believes in a divine cosmic plan that includes this present earth.	Believes in a (postponed) cosmic plan that (largely) excludes this present earth.
Disciples and has an impact in whole nations (Matthew 28:19).	Disciples individual ethnic people groups.
Has a vision for the whole community.	Has a visión for their whole congregation or denominational structure.
Aspires to influence each of the cultural spheres of society.	Aspires to function only in the sphere of "religion".

CHAPTER 6
♦♦♦

Kingdom Mindset vs. church Mindset

> "⁹Worthy are You to take the book and to break its seals; for You were slain, and purchased for God with Your blood men from every tribe and tongue and people and nation. ¹⁰ You have made them to be a kingdom and priests to our God; and they will reign upon the earth."
> Revelation 5:9-10

There is presently a revolution-taking place among those on the leading edge of change in the Evangelical "church". The result is a transition from a "church" mindset to a Kingdom (government) mindset in which the walls of "church" buildings are no longer able to contain the raw creative energy of Christ-followers who are committed to preaching and applying the Gospel of the Kingdom to all the world, including its systems and structures.

Political solutions and big government, attempts to heal our land yet they have failed miserably.

More and more people are looking to faith-based partnerships and "churches" to find solutions. Hence the irrelevancy of old "church" patterns and religious traditions will become more noticeable in the decades to come.

Consequently, it behooves us to continue to study the contrasts between cutting-edge Kingdom (government) practices and old, irrelevant religious "church" patterns that have failed to effectively evangelize and transform communities with the gospel of the Kingdom (government) of God.

The following is a contrast between leaders with a Kingdom (government) mindset and those with a traditional religious "church" mindset:

1. <u>Kingdom (government) leaders interpret Matthew 28:19-20 (*"19 Go therefore and make disciples of all the nations, baptizing them in the name of the Father and the Son and the Holy Spirit, 20 teaching them to observe all that I commanded you; and lo, I am with you always, even to the end of the age"*) as referring to discipling all nations.</u>
"Church" leaders believe it only refers to all individual ethnic peoples.

The Body of Christ is now re-thinking the Great Commission scriptures of Mark 16:15 (*"and He said to them: Go into all the world and preach the gospel to all creation"*). Instead of viewing them as commands to merely evangelize individual souls, now many are viewing the command in Mark 16 to 'go into all the world and preach' as a command to apply the gospel of the Kingdom, to both individual sinners and world systems. Matthew 28:19-20 *("19 Go therefore and make disciples of all the nations, baptizing them in the name of the*

Father and the Son and the Holy Spirit, ²⁰ teaching them to observe all that I commanded you; and lo, I am with you always, even to the end of the age") is now regarded as the New Testament equivalent to the Cultural Mandate found in Genesis 1:28 (*"God blessed them; and God said to them, "Be fruitful and multiply, and fill the earth, and subdue it; and rule over the fish of the sea and over the birds of the sky and over every living thing that moves on the earth"*).

2. <u>Kingdom (government) leaders attempt to nurture and release world-class leaders who serve their communities.</u>
"Church" leaders nurture only those who serve the various ministries of the "church" that mainly evolve around the weekly services of the ministry.

Kingdom leaders understand that only 2% to 3% of those in their congregations are called to full-time "church" ministry. The remaining 97% are called to be equipped and discipled for the work of the ministry Ephesians 4:12 (*"for the equipping of the saints for the work of service, to the building up of the body of Christ"*) which, in the Kingdom, include all areas of the community, not only ecclesial ministry. With this view, there is room for everyone in the congregation to be set apart and trained as an Ambassador of the Kingdom in every place of society.

3. <u>Kingdom (government) leaders understand and work with God's common grace.</u>
"Church" leaders only understand and work with those who have experienced saving grace.

Kingdom leaders understand that God's grace has been

poured out to all of humanity so the world can function normally. Romans 13:1-7 calls civic leaders God's ministers (diakanos or deacons):

> "¹ Every person is to be in subjection to the governing authorities. For there is no authority except from God, and those which exist are established by God. ² Therefore whoever resists authority has opposed the ordinance of God; and they who have opposed will receive condemnation upon themselves. ³ For rulers are not a cause of fear for good behavior, but for evil. Do you want to have no fear of authority? Do what is good and you will have praise from the same; ⁴ for it is a minister of God to you for good. But if you do what is evil, be afraid; for it does not bear the sword for nothing; for it is a minister of God, an avenger who brings wrath on the one who practices evil. ⁵ Therefore it is necessary to be in subjection, not only because of wrath, but also for conscience' sake. ⁶ For because of this you also pay taxes, for rulers are servants of God, devoting themselves to this very thing. ⁷ Render to all what is due them: tax to whom tax is due; custom to whom custom; fear to whom fear; honor to whom honor."

If God calls unredeemed leaders His ministers then Kingdom leaders know they can also partner with political and community leaders, even if they are not in full agreement when it comes to faith and core values.

"Church" leaders only work with those that are in full agreement with their core religious values, thus insulating themselves from the world around them.

4. <u>Kingdom (government) leaders have a biblical worldview that encompasses all of life.</u>
"Church" leaders have a semi-gnostic Greek view of Scripture that regards only spiritual things as important.

Kingdom leaders know that the earth is the Lord's and not the devil's (Psalm 24). They know that the Word became flesh (*"And the Word became flesh, and dwelt among us, and we saw His glory, glory as of the only begotten from the Father, full of grace and truth"*, **John 1:14**). Thus, the material world is also sacred and something to be cultivated (*"Then the Lord God took the man and put him into the garden of Eden to cultivate it and keep it"*, **Genesis 2:15**).
"Church" leaders are only concerned with spiritual things like prayer, healing, the gifts and fruit of the Spirit, etc. These spiritual things are only really effective if they are applied to our walk with God and its concomitant love of neighbor as salt and light.

5. <u>Kingdom (government) leaders are working towards a new Christendom (ekklessia).</u>
"Church" leaders are only trying to produce individual Christians.

Kingdom leaders desire to interweave the principles of God's Word into every fabric of culture so every nation and city favors Christianity and bases civic laws on biblical precepts.

"Church" leaders are not overly concerned with politics and economics but with adding new converts who, without a biblical worldview, will only perpetuate humanistic ungodly systems with their partial "spiritual" gospel.

6. <u>Kingdom (government) leaders teach the ekklesía to embrace their secular communities before they experience conversion.</u>
"Church" leaders embrace people into their faith communities only after they experience salvation.

Kingdom leaders regard their cities and communities as gifts to the ekklesía and to the people who live in them. They embrace their communities in humility and send their members into their communities as servant leaders who will be the greatest problem solvers of the most challenging human needs.
"Church" leaders only embrace individuals in their communities after they have professed faith in Jesus. Thus, they insulate and isolate themselves and their "churches" from the felt needs of their communities, yet are joyful as long as their "churches" are growing and their bills are paid.

7. <u>Kingdom (government) leaders turn the world upside down ("*When they did not find them, they began dragging Jason and some brethren before the city authorities, shouting, "These men who have upset the world have come here also*", Acts 17:6).</u>
"Church" leaders restructure their local "churches".

In Acts 17 it was said, when the apostles came into a community that "*...these men who have upset the world have*

come here also".
Nowadays the typical "church" mindset is only concerned with what happens within the four walls of the "church" building. There are many "churches" that, if they closed down, the local city councils, police stations, courthouses, businesses and political leaders would barely notice they were gone.

8. <u>Kingdom (government) leaders articulate Christ as Lord over every culture.</u>
"Church" leaders preach Christ as only the head of the "church".

Kingdom leaders recognize Jesus place as King of every secular king. This has vast cultural and political implications, and pressures the ekklesía to engage the secular arena.
Those with a "church" mindset only preach Jesus as the head of the "church" and neglect Christ function as King over the unredeemed world.

9. <u>Kingdom (government) leaders shepherd whole communities.</u>
"Church" leaders shepherd only the members of their congregations.

Kingdom leaders understand they are called to communities, not only to local "churches". Hence, they see themselves as shepherds and spiritual leaders of regions.
"Church" leaders feel no responsibility to their communities because they feel committed only to those who are members and have faithful attendance to their weekly ser-

vices.

10. <u>Kingdom (government) leaders believe in spiritual warfare between the kingdom of darkness and the kingdom of light and how the battle is not against flesh and blood but against spiritual forces</u> (*"For our struggle is not against flesh and blood, but against the rulers, against the powers, against the world forces of this darkness, against the spiritual forces of wickedness in the heavenly places"*, **Ephesians 6:12**). These spiritual forces are producing the ungodly social systems we have in our communities.
Some "church" leaders only cast out evil spirits out of individual people. Others do not believe in deliverance.

Kingdom leaders understand that Jesus came to redeem systemic evil, not just individual sin (*"and through Him to reconcile all things to Himself, having made peace through the blood of His cross; through Him, I say, whether things on earth or things in heaven"*, **Colossians 1:20**).
"Church" leaders only feel called to deal with individual evil. Thus, they interpret passages such as Luke 4:18 as dealing with the individual poor and oppressed, neglecting the systemic reference from which it came. (Read Isaiah 61:1-4 to see that Luke 4:18 *("The Spirit of the Lord is upon Me, Because He anointed Me to preach the gospel to the poor. He has sent Me to proclaim release to the captives, And recovery of sight to the blind, To set free those who are oppressed")* concerns redeeming and restoring desolate cities, not just individuals in need.

11. <u>Kingdom (government) leaders pray for God's will to be done on earth as it is in heaven.</u>

"Church" leaders pray for revival in their "churches".
The Lord's Prayer (*"Your kingdom come. Your will be done, On earth as it is in heaven"*, Matthew 6:10) teaches us to pray that God's Kingdom (government) come and His will be done on earth as it is in heaven.

Thus, Kingdom leaders have as their prayer focus the Kingdom (government) being manifest on the earth daily. Leaders with a "Church" mindset are content with meetings and events, where there are various moves of the spirit, signs and wonders. Instead of striving for a manifestation of the Kingdom (government) in their cities that impacts the quality of life politically and economically (Isaiah 61:3-4).

12. <u>Kingdom (government) leaders believe for the gospel to economically lift whole communities.</u>
"Church" leaders believe for greater tithes and offerings to support their building projects and "church" programs.

13. <u>Kingdom (government) leaders gravitate toward the complexities and challenges of cities.</u>
"Church" leaders gravitate toward lives of isolation and inward focus.

Before the Civil War, when the American ekklesía preached the Kingdom message, the ekklesía was able to draft the founding documents of this great nation, and start schools and Ivy League universities, all for the purpose of placing godly leaders in society as the future presidents, governors, mayors, scientists, artists, writers, etc. The ekklesía took the lead in cultural reform.

But after the horrible experiences of the Civil War the ekklesía lost hope in the Kingdom being manifest on the earth and started to focus on the imminent return of Christ and the rapture. This resulted in American culture being lost to secularists in one generation.

This turning away from the Kingdom (government) message led to "church" leaders isolating themselves from the looming threats of biblical higher criticism, Marxism, Darwinism, the infiltration of non-WASP immigrants, Sigmund Freud and psychology, and the Industrial Revolution. These brought many pressures upon the nuclear family as men had to go into the cities to find work.

Instead of engaging the culture and these challenges head-on, the American "church" started looking for escape and changed its theology. The present move of God is finally bringing the "church" back onto the biblical footing of the Kingdom (government) message.

14. Kingdom (government) leaders equip people for Kingdom life.
"Church" leaders equip people for "church" life.

Kingdom leaders inspire and equip the saints to serve in their cities as salt and light, to be like Daniel and Joseph who prospered and held significant leadership roles in the midst of pagan systems and kings.
"Church" leaders train people to be preachers, teachers singers, worship leaders, associate pastor's, counselors, ushers, leaders of various ministries within the "church", cell group leaders, for multiplication and "church" growth.

15. <u>Kingdom (government) leaders honor Jesus dual role as Redeemer and Creator.</u>
"Church" leaders separate redemption from creation.

Kingdom leaders realize that the Jesus who died on the cross (*"For God so loved the world, that He gave His only begotten Son, that whoever believes in Him shall not perish, but have eternal life"*, **John 3:16**) for the sins of the world (*"he next day he saw Jesus coming to him and said, "Behold, the Lamb of God who takes away the sin of the world."* **John 1:29**) is the same Jesus who created the world (*"³ All things came into being through Him, and apart from Him nothing came into being that has come into being. ⁴ In Him was life, and the life was the Light of men"*, **John 1:3-4**) **and** was born to be KING and LORD of ALL.

When we apply the Word of God to culture we are embracing Christ ownership of the whole world. But when we preach the cross of Jesus only for individual sinners and do not also apply it to the created order we separate the Redeemer from the Creator.

16. <u>Kingdom (government) leaders are forward thinkers. New wineskin.</u>
"Church" leaders long for the past and are old wineskin. And cannot receive the New Wine of the Kingdom.

Kingdom leaders are excited about the future advance of Christendom in every facet of life and for every nation. They are excited over the increasing influence of Christ in culture. They train believers to replenish the earth by placing godly leaders in the realms of science, art, media, education, economics and politics. The sky is the limit for them.

Those with a "church" mindset long for the past, when life was much simpler and everyone in a community embraced the role of Christianity in culture. They do not like the vast complexities that social fragmentation has presented because it distracts from, and interferes with, their nice and neat "church" and parish structures.

17. <u>Kingdom (government) leaders know that they have been chosen to reign and rule on earth</u> (*"You have made them to be a kingdom and priests to our God; and they will reign upon the earth"*, **Revelation 5:10**).
"Church" leaders are focused on escaping the earth and making it to heaven.

The Bible is essentially not a book about heaven. It is not concerned with another geographic location whether spiritual or physical. It is mainly concerned with the person of Christ and His rule and dominion in the cosmos:

> "⁹ He made known to us the mystery of His will, according to His kind intention which He purposed in Him ¹⁰ with a view to an administration suitable to the fullness of the times, that *is*, the summing up of all things in Christ, things in the heavens and things on the earth. In Him ¹¹ also we have obtained an inheritance, having been predestined according to His purpose who works all things after the counsel of His will." Ephesians 1:9-11

Because of this, the Bible is the most practical book about life on the earth that has ever been written.

Kingdom (government) leaders understand and embrace this reality.
"Church" leaders emphasize heaven since they have no real sense of purpose to give to the majority of their congregants who are not called into full-time "church" ministry.

18. <u>Kingdom (government) leaders envision the building of universities with the gospel of the Kingdom serving as the "queen of the sciences".</u>
"Church" leaders envision the establishment of church-centered Bible institutes and seminaries that avoid liberal arts and the humanities.

19. <u>Kingdom (government) leaders are entrepreneurs.</u>
"Church" leaders are stuck in maintenance mode, merely holding their ground until Christ comes back, or they make it to heaven.

20. <u>Kingdom (government) leaders pray for revival that brings men and women to be discipled and equipped as leaders in a world system.</u>
"Church" leaders merely pray and believe for higher attendance in their weekly meetings.

21. <u>Kingdom (government) leaders work for cultural transformation.</u>
"Church" leaders focus on waiting for the second coming of Christ so they can escape the apocalypse of this world.
Jesus told the "church" to occupy until He comes.

Kingdom (government) leaders are busy strategizing how they are going to start schools of government to train political candidates, start businesses to create wealth to expand the Kingdom (government), and develop educational programs to break cycles of poverty for at-risk children.
Those with a "church" mindset do not get involved in quality of life issues because their theology doesn't allow for it. They think it is like arranging the chairs on the Titanic because the world will soon end when the antichrist takes over.

22. <u>Kingdom (government) leaders train their children to walk in biblical dominion in society.</u>
"Church" leaders' highest hope is that their children don't fall away from the faith.

Kingdom leaders have dominion as the primary goal for their children. They don't teach their children to get secure jobs in big companies; they teach them to become the CEOs of Fortune 500 companies. They don't teach them how to fish but how to own a lake. They echo the words of Moses in Deuteronomy 28:10-13:

> "[10] So all the peoples of the earth will see that you are called by the name of the Lord, and they will be afraid of you. [11] The Lord will make you abound in prosperity, in the offspring of your body and in the offspring of your beast and in the produce of your ground, in the land which the Lord swore to your fathers to give you. [12] The Lord will open for you His good storehouse, the heavens, to give rain to your

> land in its season and to bless all the work of your hand; and you shall lend to many nations, but you shall not borrow. ¹³ The Lord will make you the head and not the tail, and you only will be above, and you will not be underneath, if you listen to the commandments of the Lord your God, which I charge you today, to observe them carefully."

Here Moses teaches believers that they are called to be the head and not the tail, to be above and not beneath, to lend to many nations and not to borrow.

"Church" leaders take a defensive posture with their children by merely praying that they would not fall away from the faith. Even many who teach apologetics and biblical worldview are stuck in the "church" mindset because they are only teaching their children how to defend the faith instead of how to advance the Kingdom.

23. <u>Kingdom (government) leaders empower the poor to own the pond.</u>
"Church" leaders give the poor some fish.

Kingdom leaders understand how to break poverty mindsets over people by equipping them to create their own wealth.
"Church" leaders have an entitlement approach in which they merely feed the poor instead of equipping them to start their own businesses or work in high-level positions that will enable them to be prosperous for the sake of the Kingdom.

Jesus, John the Baptist, and the apostles went about proclaiming the Kingdom (government)–not the "church" (read Matthew 3:2, 4:17, 10:7; Acts.1:3, Acts 28:30-31). All the words of Jesus were about the Kingdom. His parables were to describe the Kingdom. Jesus never taught Judaism or any religion.

Kingdom denotes 'the rule of God over the whole cosmos', not just a single entity on the earth, like the "church". In spite of this, most preaching today has as its goal to get people to make a weekly two-hour commitment to come to a building for a "worship service" and to give tithes and offerings to support that building and religious structure. This is because a spirit of religion has captivated the "church" and blinded the minds of "church" leaders, so that we now have a very limited "church" mindset instead of a Kingdom (government) perspective.

In essence, a Kingdom (government) mindset regards Christianity as a biblical world and life view centered on the person of Jesus Christ who is Lord of all creation. This has vast political, economic, and sociological implications.

Those with a "church" mindset view Jesus merely as the King of the "church", not the King of all earthly secular kings.

The following are contrasts between these two mindsets:

KINGDOM	CHURCH
Releases all saints as ministers in the marketplace.	Merely trains people to serve in a "church" building on.
Creates wealth to transform a community and nation.	Motivates giving to build "church" programs and grow the organization or denomination around the world.
Is a holistic approach that integrates the gospel with politics, economics, and public policy.	Insulates the gospel from politics and public policy.
Views the Bible as a blueprint to structure every aspect of society.	Views the Bible merely as a pietistic book that enables us to escape the world, enter heaven, and be spiritual.
Embraces and loves their surrounding unchurched communities.	Only embraces converted individuals within their faith communities.
Trains people for all of life.	Trains people only for "church" life.
Nurtures leaders who are world changers and "cultural creative's" who articulate truth to society.	Nurtures leaders who speak religious language relevant only to "church" people.

KINGDOM	CHURCH
Speaks of the rule of God over the entire created order.	Speaks of the rule of God through deacons and elders over those in a "church" congregation.
Shepherds and leaders release their people to their vocational callings in the marketplace.	Controls people by marginalizing their marketplace callings and emphasizing only their individual "church" ministries.
Applies a Spirit-empowered approach to the natural world.	Involves a spirituality that separates from the natural world.
Are working toward a renaissance of Christendom.	Merely strive for a particular expression (denomination) of Christianity.
Equip 100% of the saints to fill all things in every realm of life (Ephesians 4:10-12).	Have as their primary goal to equip the 2-3% of the congregation called to be full-time "church" pastors, ministers, and missionaries.

CONCLUSION
♦♦♦

"²⁴ Then comes the end, when He hands over the kingdom to the God and Father, when He has abolished all rule and all authority and power. ²⁵ For He must reign until He has put all His enemies under His feet."
1 Corinthians 15:24-25

Throughout this book we have seen God's eternal purpose to establish His KINGDOM (government) on Earth. He created man for this purpose:

> **The invisible God created a visible man, so that through the visible man, the invisible God could govern the visible earth with the invisible Eternal Government.**

Man disobeyed the first order that The Lord gave him and failed to fulfill the purpose for which he had been created (*"¹⁶ The Lord God commanded the man, saying, "From any tree of the garden you may eat freely; ¹⁷ but from the tree of the knowledge of good and evil you shall not eat, for in the day that you eat from it you will surely die"*, **Genesis 2:16-17**).

Tradition has told us, that Adam fell into sin, yet I've shown you that it was sin that made man fall from the purpose for which God created him, to subdue the Earth.

Tho man fell from his original purpose, God did not abandon His eternal plan of establishing His Kingdom (government) on Earth.

Man, after falling from the purpose and with the sentence of eternal death (*"Therefore, just as through one man sin entered into the world, and death through sin, and so death spread to all men, because all sinned"*, **Romans 5:12**) needs to be redeemed from his spiritual condition with the government of God. The problem of Adam and his descendants with God is not a religious issue, but a governmental issue.

Therefore, God Himself provides man with the solution for his judicial problem with the government of God, sending His Son Jesus as savior and redeemer.

The death of Jesus on the cross of Calvary provides man with the solution to his governmental issue with God.

This is why every human being, who by faith receives Jesus as Savior, Redeemer and Lord, is delivered from the sentence imposed by the judicial system of the Government of God.

In Christ, man can be created again and be restored to the original purpose for which God created him in the beginning.

Christ rose as KING of KINGS and LORD of LORDS to sit at the right hand of the Father to rule this Earth.

Before ascending He left us the Governor, in the person of the Holy Spirit and through Him the principles and truths of the Kingdom (government) are revealed.

As we submit to the Lordship of Christ, God's will is fulfilled in our lives. Thus, the Holy Spirit governs and shows us how to establish the kingdom (government) of God on Earth.

The Old Testament prophesies speak and reveal to us what was to happen in the future. The birth of Jesus is announced in Isaiah 9:

> "For unto us a Child is born, unto us a Son is given: and the government shall be upon His shoulder: and His Name shall be called Wonderful, Counselor, The Mighty God, The Everlasting Father, The Prince of Peace. Of the increase of His government and peace there shall be no end, upon the throne of David, and upon His kingdom, to order it, and to establish it with judgment and with justice from henceforth even forever." Isaiah 9:6-7

This passage states that the GOVERNMENT would be put on his shoulders and the increase of his government (authority) would never end.

In the same way, in the book of Daniel all the prophecies revolve around the KINGDOM, which would be established after the empires and kingdoms of this world.

We have seen in all the chapters of this book that the vocabulary of the Bible is about the Kingdom and government of God.

When Jesus begins his ministry, his first words are: "THE KINGDOM OF HEAVEN IS AT HAND".

> "From that time Jesus began to preach and say, Repent, for the kingdom of heaven is at hand."
> Matthew 4:17

All His parables taught the principles and spiritual truths of the KINGDOM.

When He, spoke to His disciples in Matthew 16:13-20, He said: "*upon this rock I will build my EKKLESÍA*". Jesus in that moment was thinking about establishing the KINGDOM (government) of God here on Earth.

When He was before Pilate, being accused of blasphemy, His words and responses all related to the KINGDOM:

> "[33] Therefore Pilate entered again into the Praetorium, and summoned Jesus and said to Him,

The Unknown Gospel

> "Are You the King of the Jews?" ³⁴ Jesus answered, "Are you saying this on your own initiative, or did others tell you about Me?" ³⁵ Pilate answered, "I am not a Jew, am I? Your own nation and the chief priests delivered You to me; what have You done?" ³⁶ Jesus answered, "My kingdom is not of this world. If My kingdom were of this world, then My servants would be fighting so that I would not be handed over to the Jews; but as it is, My kingdom is not of this realm." ³⁷ Therefore Pilate said to Him, "So You are a king?" Jesus answered, "You say correctly that I am a king. For this I have been born, and for this I have come into the world, to testify to the truth. Everyone who is of the truth hears My voice." John 18:33-37

In His final 40 days before ascending, Christ was teaching his disciples everything concerning the things of the KINGDOM (*"To these He also presented Himself alive after His suffering, by many convincing proofs, appearing to them over a period of forty days and speaking of the things concerning the kingdom of God"*, Acts 1:3).

The apostles, according to how they had been commissioned, taught the gospel of the Kingdom (government).

The book of Acts ends with Paul renting a house and teaching about the KINGDOM:

> "³⁰ And he stayed two full years in his own rented quarters and was welcoming all who came to

him, ³¹ preaching the kingdom of God and teaching concerning the Lord Jesus Christ with all openness, unhindered." Acts 28:30-31

The books of Isaiah, Daniel, Acts and Revelation speak of the KINGDOM, the triumph of the KING and his KINGDOM (government) along with all the royal priesthood who will rule with Him on Earth.

As we can see, the whole Bible is about God's eternal purpose of establishing His KINGDOM (government) on Earth.

However, in the 21st century the world is filled with RELIGION and not the authority of the Kingdom of God.

There are millions of "churches", religions, cults, ecclesiastical systems, denominations, apostolic networks, charismatic and pentecostal movements, yet very little KINGDOM (government).

As never before, in many countries and continents of the Earth there is an open persecution against God, His Word and His spiritual laws. Man's systems have not brought about the will of God.

Many false apostles, prophets, teachers, evangelists, and pastors are preaching a gospel full of religious tradition that only has produced large meetings, conferences, events and supposed revivals that have only been for the glory of man.

These have produced a people who are perishing in spiritual and physical death ("*My people are destroyed for lack of knowledge...*", Hosea 4:6).

Jesus said in Matthew 16: 18-19:

> "¹⁸ I also say to you that you are Peter, and upon this rock I will build My "church"; and the gates of Hades will not overpower it. ¹⁹ I will give you the keys of the kingdom of heaven; and whatever you bind on earth shall have been bound in heaven, and whatever you loose on earth hall have been loosed in heaven."

To use the keys of the kingdom we must understand Matthew 6:9-13. Jesus teaches us to pray "THY KINGDOM COME".

Religious tradition has taught us that these words have to do with the second coming of Christ; however, Jesus longed for us to understand the need to ask daily for the GOVERNMENT of God to come and rule our lives.

Certainly, we have a big challenge ahead.

If you're a servant of God, you need to ask yourself: what Gospel am I living, teaching and serving?

1. Is it the everlasting gospel of the Kingdom (government) of God?
   Or the gospel that religious tradition, influenced by the kingdom of darkness has taught you?

2. Are you part of the EKKLESÍA that Christ is building?
Or part of the religious system of man ("church")?

3. Are you a citizen of the Kingdom?
Or a member of a religious system ("church")?

4. Are you an ambassador of Christ and His Kingdom (government) in the spheres where God has placed you? Or are you just serving or ministering in religious services?

5. What principles govern your daily life? Those of the Kingdom (government) of God?
Or the theologies, doctrines, dogmas and rules of a religious system?

6. Does your vocabulary confess a Kingdom mindset?
Or a religious "church" mindset?

> "[6] And He said to them, "Rightly did Isaiah prophesy of you hypocrites, as it is written:'This people honors Me with their lips, But their heart is far away from Me. [7] 'But in vain do they worship Me, Teaching as doctrines the precepts of men.' [8] Neglecting the commandment of God, you hold to the tradition of men." [9] He was also saying to them, "You are experts at setting aside the commandment of God in order to keep your tradition." Mark 7:6-9

I pray, that the Holy Spirit will lead you and enlighten you to answer these questions.

The word of God is very explicit and reveals to us the ETERNAL GOSPEL OF THE KINGDOM OF GOD. He desires that you know this Gospel. This book is the first of a series about the Kingdom and the life in the KINGDOM.